The Racing Schooner
Westward

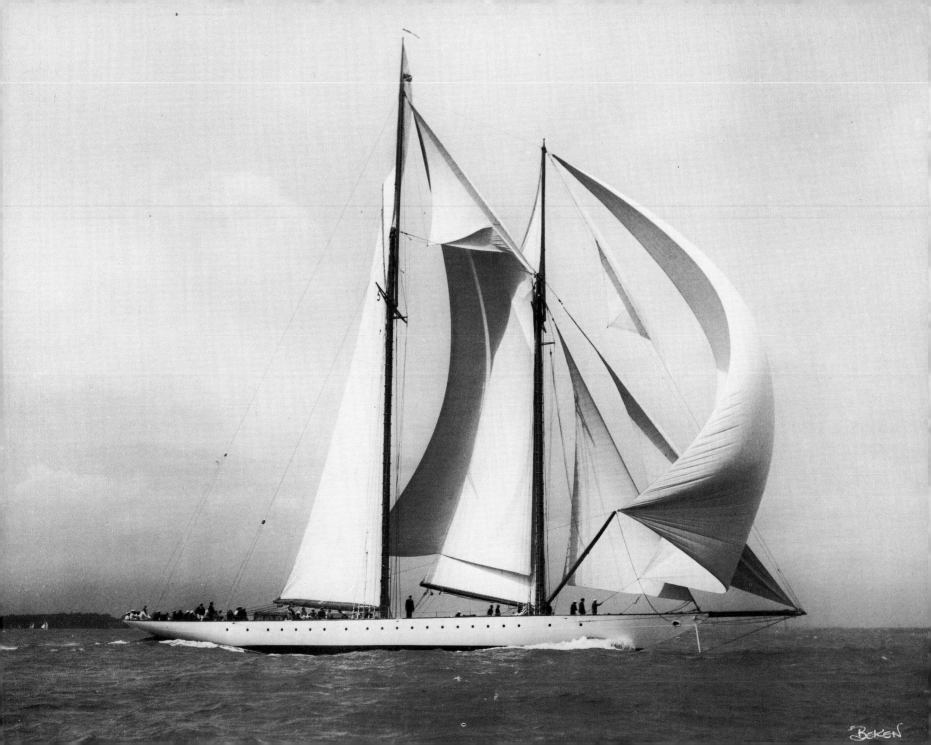

# The Racing Schooner
# Westward

C P Hamilton-Adams

VNR VAN NOSTRAND REINHOLD COMPANY

NEW YORK   CINCINNATI   TORONTO   LONDON   MELBOURNE

*First published in Great Britain 1976*
*by Stanford Maritime Limited*
*12 Long Acre, London WC2E 9LP*

*Copyright © C P Hamilton-Adams 1976*
*Library of Congress Catalog Card Number 76-50429*
*ISBN 0-442-23087-7*

**Published in the USA 1977 by Van Nostrand Reinhold Company**
**A division of Litton Educational Publishing, Inc.**
**450 West 33rd Street, New York, NY 10001**

*16  15  14  13  12  11  10  9  8  7  6  5  4  3  2  1*

*To Joan in all her help*

# Preface

On July 15, 1947 *Westward*, one of the most beautiful racing schooners ever to be created, slipped beneath the waters of the English Channel, to rest forever on the seabed in the Hurd Deep. She left as she had arrived, surrounded by controversy.

Further out in the Channel, in the direction of St Catherine's Point, lies an even more famous yacht, King George V's *Britannia*. Although the royal cutter was senior by seventeen years, the two had had much in common, and in a wind of Force 5 or above they could usually be relied upon to give the rest of the fleet a run for their money. On one hundred and seventy-four occasions they raced together around the coasts of Britain, watched and admired by thousands of people not remotely interested in yachting but intrigued by the beauty and grandeur of their passing.

That these two yachts were rivals, despite the fact that one was a Clyde-built cutter launched in 1893 and the other an American schooner built in 1909–10, was undoubtedly true; and one has only to remember the epic race between them in a gale of wind in 1932 to confirm this assumption. It was *Britannia*'s weather with a vengeance, a full gale from the southwest with driving rain so heavy that on occasions one could only see a few yards ahead of the bowsprit. The King was aboard *Britannia*, the rest of the fleet either far astern or retired, so for forty-five miles the two yachts fought it out together. As they cleared the lee of the Isle of Wight and felt the full force of the Channel gale, *Westward* due to her large spread of canvas became almost unmanageable, needing the full strength of three men at the wheel to keep her on course. Eventually they stormed back across the finishing line at Southsea to the cheers of the crowd and in a dead heat. This was racing in the grand manner.

Over the years much has been written about the King's *Britannia*, including the splendid book by John Irving, but for some reason *Westward* has not received anything like the same acclaim. This I am now trying to rectify.

C P Hamilton-Adams

'West Wind'
Walhampton
Lymington, Hampshire

Drawings of *Westward*'s construction are reproduced from originals in the Haffenreffer-Herreshoff Collection in the Hart Nautical Museum, Massachusetts Institute of Technology

Photographs are from various sources, including the following

Beken of Cowes: jacket illustration (front) and pages 2, 6, 23, 24, 27, 42, 47, 50, 58, 62, 68, 75, 81, 84, 92, 99, 105

Drayton Cochran, Esq.: jacket illustration (back) and pages 12, 14, 17, 18, 19, 20, 21, 22, 28–34, 37, 38, 39, 52, 61, 63, 66, 69, 74

Kirk & Son, courtesy of Roger M Smith: pages 70, 73, 76, 94

Société Jersiaise: pages 55, 56, 63, 87, 100, 101, 104

N L Stebbins, courtesy of the Society for the Preservation of New England Antiquities: page 26

Ailsa Craig Ltd kindly contributed details of *Westward*'s engine installation.

# Acknowledgement

I am deeply conscious of the help which has been offered me freely by many people during the period in which this book has been in preparation, and without which the task of writing it would have been infinitely more difficult. To all of them I am deeply grateful.

Capt Barton, J R Baughan, Cdr R D Bayliffe, R Beaumont, H Benham, C W Bond, A C Clark, Miss C Cochran, Mr Drayton Cochran, C Currey, Mrs F Davidson, J Fieldgate, C Glass, Frau Christa Gehrickens, Capt Griffith, R L Hewitt, Lt Cdr F C Hard, Capt Harris, Capt John Illingworth, R W Kennaway, Mrs Lyle, E C Larbalestier, R V D Moger, Mr Prichard, Capt W L G Porter, RN, Capt Saunders, Mrs Simpson-Smith, J Tew, J Treffry, Stephen Vagliano, Capt J V Waterhouse, G Watson-Williams.

My thanks are also due to the Hon. Secretary, Mrs W Macready, and staff of the Museum of the Société Jersiaise, and the National Maritime Museum at Greenwich, for all their help; also to J D Sleightholme, editor of *Yachting Monthly*, for articles on *Westward*.

And to Frank S Beck, one of the professional crew of *Westward*, who has seen it all.

I am particularly indebted for the forbearance of Phoebe Mason, a very patient editor, for 'vetting' the manuscript and assisting with some of the technicalities.

Mr Drayton Cochran has very kindly loaned scrapbooks and family papers which belonged to Alexander S Cochran, *Westward*'s original owner, and many of the early photographs reproduced here are from these scrapbooks.

# Chapter 1

To say that *Westward* was the most famous racing schooner in the world would of course be untrue, for the great days of schooner racing were already declining before she was launched in 1910. Nevertheless there were many contemporaries, such as the German Emperor's *Meteors*, *Iduna*, *Germania*, *Cicely*, *Hamburg*, *Clara* and *Susanna*, several schooners that never left the Baltic, and also a number on the Atlantic seaboard of America, (*Enchantress*, *Karina*, *Atlantic*, *Irolita*) all capable of giving *Westward* a hard race. Surely pride of place must be given to *America*, which sailed across the Atlantic in 1851 looking for a race. The Royal Yacht Squadron eventually offered a cup valued at one hundred guineas for a scratch race round the Isle of Wight, and with the help of a Cowes Pilot named Underwood who knew the local tides and conditions, *America* raced against seventeen yachts ranging in size from 47 tons up to 392 tons, and trounced them all. The cup went to the United States where it has remained for a hundred and twenty-five years, and the chance of winning it back seems as remote as ever.

So we can commence by saying that *Westward* was undoubtedly the best known racing schooner ever to come to Britain, for she raced season after season between 1910 and 1938 at most of the large regattas around the coast, in company with *Britannia*, *Astra*, *Cambria*, *Candida*, *Lulworth*, *Shamrock IV* and *White Heather*, and highly developed J Class boats such as *Shamrock V*, *Endeavour*, *Velsheda* and *Yankee*. Beside the cutters mentioned above, in her first season she also had to meet five formidable schooners: *Germania*, *Hamburg*, *Meteor IV*, *Cicely* and *Susanna*. Highly tuned and very competitive, they had raced many times together and knew each other's good and bad points of sailing, and the local waters, and were all looking forward to the 1910 season to see if the new 'Herreshoff flyer' (as the press called *Westward*) was as good as had been forecast.

*Westward*, schooner, steel. 323 tons, LOA 135 ft, LWL 96 ft 1 in, breadth 27 ft 1 in, draft 16 ft 9 in, sail area 12,000 sq ft: such figures can be obtained from any edition of *Lloyd's Register of Yachts* from 1910 to 1947. What is more important is to look much deeper and to find out what sort of ship she really was, and more important still, what the people were like who conceived her design and turned their thoughts into reality.

To do so one must go back as far as 1790, when Frederick Herreshoff left Germany to migrate to the United States of America and settle on Prudence Island in Rhode Island, there to become a farmer, eventually marrying Sarah Brown, the daughter of a shipbuilder from Rhode Island. There have since been several generations of Herreshoffs, a name that was to become and remain famous in yachting, in somewhat the same way as Nicholson's in Europe. Unfortunately, due to some genetic failing the Herreshoffs had constant trouble with their eyesight, suffering from an obscure form of glaucoma, several children having been born blind, and this fate hung over the whole family.

The two Herreshoffs who were connected with *Westward* were John and his younger brother Nathanael. They were fascinated by boats from childhood, and as they lived on the water's edge it was not long before John built himself a catboat which he sailed in the local regattas. At the age of fifteen, he was suddenly struck totally blind, but fought back and even continued racing his boat, with his younger brother Nat, then age nine,

as lookout. As the boys started to grow up, there came a temporary parting of the ways. Nat decided to become a mechanical engineer and graduated from Massachusetts Institute of Technology in 1869, while John still built catboats, forming a little company of his own, and despite his blindness worked in the wood shop whenever he could. All well known figures have stories told about them, and they no doubt improve on the telling, but the following story is so persistent that it could be true. Although eventually acclaimed in America and abroad as one of the leading designers of all time, Nat never started a large project like *Westward* without first having a model of his new design made out of wood for John, who would sit with it on his knees and gently stroke it, criticizing its line and shape if such criticism was necessary. It is said that Nat was never really happy until John had given his new brainchild his blessing.

In 1876 Nat the engineer and John the shipwright formed the Herreshoff Manufacturing Co. of Bristol, Rhode Island, making fast steam launches as well as yachts; what was once a hobby now became a business. In time John became the business executive and Nat the designer, whose skill and reputation grew rapidly over the years. Before the launch of *Westward* and despite the constant production of steam launches, tenders, catboats and dinghies, many vessels passed down the slipways, including thirty-eight fast sailing cruisers, other racing yachts, and steam torpedo boats for the US Navy. Some were destined for Britain—the smallest of these the little Half Rater *Wee Win* that was to be seen for many years racing around the Solent. (Although she was usually based at Bembridge on the Isle of Wight, *Wee Win* was often to be seen at Cowes,

*Westward was launched on March 31, 1910 at eleven o'clock and christened by Mrs A Livingstone Beekman.*

and was greatly admired by Uffa Fox; some say that it influenced his thinking when designing his famous Flying Fifteen many years later.) Well before *Westward* was commissioned, the Herreshoffs had become world famous for building the defenders of the America's Cup, and for the breadth of their yacht and boat building expertise and engineering. To close this chapter, I feel I could not do better than to quote the late Uffa Fox in his book *Sail and Power*: 'Having studied the designs with which Fife and Nicholson, the two great artists, endeavoured to win the America's Cup, it is interesting to take a peep at the other side of the Atlantic. Not only did Nathanael Greene Herreshoff design *Reliance* (1903) and *Resolute* (1920), but he designed the defenders which turned back all six challenges from 1893 to 1920. One cannot but be amazed at the ability of one man, whose designs competed successfully against those of three great masters, G L Watson, William Fife and Charles E Nicholson.'

Yes, *Westward* undoubtedly came from the right stable.

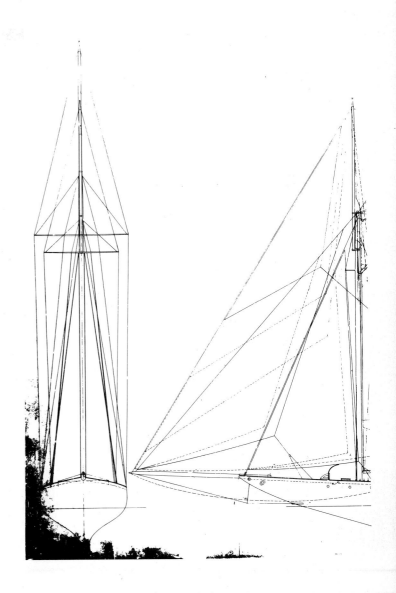

*Moored off the Herreshoff yard during her work-up in April 1910. Several large yachts are laid up under covers on shore, to protect them from ice.*

# Chapter 2

Mr Alexander S Cochran of East 41st Street in New York was a rich and successful man with a taste for yachting, art and polo, and determined that his new schooner would be equally successful. Giving the Herreshoffs the commission was a shrewd move, for he knew that they were on their way up; *Westward* was the largest sailing yacht in terms of waterline length that they had built, and the first to the International Rule of 1908 (despite its name, not adopted in America), and they were keen to take on the challenge. The owner gave *carte blanche* for the purchase of the best of equipment, and expense was secondary. Thus a complete set of sails was ordered from Ratsey & Lapthorn in England, then considered the best sailmakers in the world (who had once refused to make sails for an earlier American yacht racing in England, after her original suit so lost their shape that she became beatable) though the Herreshoff Manufacturing Co. made sails, as well as deck gear, ironwork, rigging fittings, winches, etc and provided some of her canvas.

The solid masts were made from selected Oregon pine, and the mainmast when finished and stepped weighed four tons with its rigging and ironwork. The keel lead has been reported to weigh around seventy-five to eighty tons; certainly she could carry her huge spread of canvas better than any schooner of similar dimensions. The hull was steel and the decks pine over the plating, with teak covering boards and rail. The standing rigging was massive by any standards; the running gear kept as simple as possible, for handling a racing schooner in the mêlée before a start is much more difficult than a cutter.

Design work began in the autumn of 1909; hull number 692 was launched on March 31, 1910 with the usual ceremonies.

To have a new boat, perfectly constructed, is one thing, but like a violin, it has to be tuned and 'played in'; Alexander Cochran had already thought on these matters, and consistent with the policy that only the

*Alexander Cochran at the helm, with Captain Barr*

Captain Charles Barr was accepted among the yachting fraternity as probably one of the finest racing skippers to be found anywhere in Europe or America, and to get such a reputation needs consistent success. He was a neatly built, dapper man of medium height, with a waxed moustache in the French fashion and a liking for cigars, which he smoked clenched firmly in his teeth even when racing. A Scot from Gourock who took up residence in America for some time, what he did not know about yacht racing and big-yacht seamanship could have been written on the back of a postage stamp. If there is need of further proof of his ability, it was he who sent *Shamrock I, II* and *III* back across the Atlantic to Britain with their tails between their legs, after challenging for the America's Cup. Barr was also blessed with a very retentive memory, and before a race would look at the courses, signals and sailing instructions and never have to refer to them again. There were no cockpits equipped with performance instruments in 1910; on a schooner the skipper had eight and sometimes ten sails to watch, and his eyes had to be everywhere.

As soon as *Westward* was launched, Charlie Barr and a hand-picked crew of thirty-one strong young men took her away to work her up; the sails had arrived from England and had to be carefully stretched in light breezes until not a wrinkle was to be seen anywhere. The crew were drilled and drilled again for every emergency, until he was satisfied that not only did they know the schooner from truck to keel, but that they worked not just as a team but almost like one man. Once he was satisfied, the beautiful racing sails were taken off and carefully stowed below decks, a squaresail for running and fore and main storm trysails taken on

best was good enough for *Westward*, he again engaged the services of Charlie Barr. A professional, Barr was also a personal friend; they had sailed together many times in Cochran's racing cutter *Avenger,* and although they came from different backgrounds had deep respect for each other's ability. In fact it was Barr who had persuaded his friend to invest in a racing schooner, and whose experience in racing the Herreshoff schooner *Ingomar* against the German and English fleets in 1904 had enhanced the attractiveness of the idea.

The passage from Brenton Reef light vessel to the Scilly Isles took thirteen days, three hours, fifty minutes. The Lizard light was abeam at 0730 and they reached the Needles at 2230 that night. After standing off and on until dawn, they entered the Solent, and were towed into dock in Southampton at 0900. The passage had taken fourteen days and the log registered 2833 nautical miles; the best day's run was 272 miles and the worst 116, giving an average for the crossing of 202 miles per day.

May 1910 was a busy time for *Westward* and her crew, as she had to be retuned after her Atlantic crossing. Most of this work was done off Portland, using

board, and with her owner and a friend aboard left the coast of America for Southampton, England on April 23, 1910.

The crossing was rough but uneventful, but enlivened by the fact that Mr Cochran suddenly decided to give up smoking, something he had tried to do many times before on medical advice, due to a history of tuberculosis. Cigarettes were his vice, and to satisfy his doctors he had them specially made from some mild form of tobacco; there was a large stock on board to carry him through his three months' absence in Europe. On the third day out from New York he ordered them all to be thrown overboard; history does not record the withdrawal symptoms, or whether Charlie Barr, seeing his friend's suffering, gave him an occasional cigar, but it is recorded that on arrival at Southampton the first thing he did was to send his steward ashore to the nearest tobacconist. He remained a heavy smoker until his death eighteen years later.

the harbour for anchoring every night. On May 26 she returned to Southampton and went into drydock for a scrub as well as to be officially measured to obtain her rating for the Kiel Regatta. The rest of the month was spent in racing drill, trying out sails and getting used to the Solent and its complex tides. At 1530 on June 14 she left Cowes bound for Cuxhaven, passing the Elbe lightship at 2100 on June 16 and anchoring off Cuxhaven at 0100 on June 17.

On arrival Cochran received the usual cordial welcome from the yacht clubs and the Norddeutschen Regatta Verein. Collected here were the finest fleet of racing schooners to be found anywhere in the world, mostly German owned.

Kaiser Wilhelm II had deliberately encouraged the development of the sport of yachting as a part of a broader plan to increase his country's maritime consciousness and stimulate enthusiasm for the German Navy, which would need strengthening in order to fulfill its role in world expansion. Participation in the bigger classes became socially advantageous; the smaller ones multiplied their numbers dramatically and helped to provide a wider interest in yachting and the talent for bigger boats, though Wilhelm admitted privately that it had taken him years to train a German crew to the standard of the British professionals. In the absence of a long-standing tradition of yacht design and construction, successful boats were purchased, studied, measured and sailed in competition with their German-built descendants.

Of the Big Class yachts racing up until the outbreak of war, many had been British. The Emperor's first *Meteor* was built in 1887 in steel by D & W Henderson on the Clyde to a design by George Watson for James

Bell of the Clyde Yacht Club. Named *Thistle*, she was a black-hulled clipper-bowed cutter, intended as an America's Cup challenger and famous in her day. *Meteor II* was another Watson cutter, built on the Clyde in 1896 and around 236 tons TM. *Meteor III* was a 130 foot steel schooner, built in New York in 1902 for the Kaiser, and designed by A Cary Smith, the most experienced designer of American big yachts. She raced at Cowes, but met *Westward* only in the Baltic, after she had been sold and renamed *Nordstern*. Her successor was *Meteor IV*, designed by Max Oertz and built in steel at Germania Werft in Kiel, and given German-made sails. She was 129 feet overall. *Lloyds Register* lists her in 1909, and this is the most frequently quoted date.

The Emperor's idea of owning a Herreshoff schooner ended when he asked to see the drawings in order to determine what changes would be necessary. Instead, the last of the series was designed by Oertz and built by Krupps in 1914 as *Meteor V*. She was the largest, being 156 feet overall, beam 25 feet, draft 18 feet, 270 tons displacement, 132 tons ballast. Although intended to compete against *Margherita*, a very fast, new schooner and one of the last of the class to be built in England, she never left German waters and had only sailed trial races against *Meteor IV* before war broke out.

In 1910 the German fleet also included *Hamburg*, ex *Rainbow*, 133 feet overall, 331 tons TM. A handsome black Watson schooner, she had sailed in the 1905

Atlantic race, and was very fast, being reputed to have logged sixteen knots for two hours. In 1914 her syndicate of owners sold her back to Britain; she was then sailed out to the Indian Ocean and the Pacific, and finally wrecked on the coast of China in 1918. *Germania*, designed by Oertz, was owned by Herr Krupp Von Bohlen und Halbach, and built by Krupps in 1908. She was 122 feet overall and 368 tons TM.

As *Westward* was being prepared for the racing it soon became apparent that although all seemed well on the surface, there remained an undercurrent of unpleasantness at Kiel that was hard to define. The Kaiser was deeply jealous of British maritime successes; *Westward*,

as had other American yachts, also suffered from this phobia. Unfortunately for everybody, and yachting in particular, Wilhelm became more and more arrogant and tiresome as the years rolled by, not only in German waters but at Cowes as well. This aggressiveness seemed to have infected some of the other competitors, but of course this could be excused under the heading of over-keenness.

On July 29 *Westward*, jockeying before the start, was closehauled on the starboard tack when *Nordstern* approached her on port; having right of way, Charlie Barr maintained his course and speed, knowing that in a crisis *Westward* could handle like a 6 Metre. The German bore down, expecting her to give way, but they did not allow for Barr, who just carried on as if the other vessel did not exist; at the very last moment he spun the wheel, taking the impact as a glancing blow on the main rigging and steel boom, and the German retired with a snapped-off bowsprit and a badly sprung mast. (Similar incidents had occurred when Barr raced *Ingomar* at Kiel in 1904.) Despite the size of the yachts, competition was just as fierce in 1910 as it is today, when every second counts, and during one of the Kiel Regatta races Barr kept *Westward* running by the lee for over thirty miles rather than sacrifice time in gybing her.

By the end of *Westward*'s brief visit to the Baltic she had outsailed and outmanoeuvred every ship in the German schooner fleet. Her starts were good, and not only was she faster going to windward, but quicker running as well, having been designed to carry more

*Hamburg,* Germania *and* Nordstern (ex Meteor III) *at Cuxhaven before the racing.* Hamburg's *spinnaker boom is raised to the vertical against the foremast.*

*Steamer with spectators at Kiel, 1910. A deckhand is walking inboard along the schooner's bowsprit, and the maintopmast-staysail is half lowered.*

Week, was placed in the A Class where she had no competition and had to sail over the course. (This was perhaps due to her past success against German schooners.) In the four main Kiel races for A1 Class yachts, *Westward* took three firsts and one fourth place, and *Meteor IV* one first and a second. The corrected times (hours, minutes, seconds) are as follows:

|  | June 25 | June 27 | June 29 | June 30 |
|---|---|---|---|---|
| *Westward* | 8.57.37 | 3.16.24 | 4.27.17 | 3.56.41 |
| *Meteor IV* | 10.0.25 | 3.23.56 | 4.48.54 | 3.43.9 |
| *Germania* | 10.31.47 | 3.22.38 | 4.37.11 | 3.49.33 |
| *Hamburg* | 10.9.30 | retired | 4.45.10 | 3.51.52 |
| *Nordstern* |  |  | 4.59.3 |  |

sail than the others; in light airs she was consistently outstanding.

At Kiel, Big Class racing was organized around a peculiar German subdivision of the A Class defined by the 1908 International Rule (and not intended by the IYRU) which grouped yachts rating between 23 and 27 metres in the A category and those over 27 metres in a special A1 Class; this accommodated the German schooners and *Westward*, but *Cicely*, a slightly smaller English schooner which had also sailed over for Kiel

*Nordstern at Kiel, with an unusual overlapping forestaysail*

For the last of these, from Eckernförde back to Kiel, a handicap was imposed; in the previous races placings were based on finishing times adjusted by time allowances based on measurement, but *Westward* was clearly out-performing the competition. She was now required to allow *Meteor IV* ten minutes, *Germania* five, *Hamburg* seven, and *Nordstern* twenty-five. The race was held in even heavier winds than on the previous day, with squalls and rain, and the German schooners, carrying less sail, overpowered her: in those conditions the handicap was not necessary to achieve the desired balance of results, and *Meteor* finished first, *Westward* coming in third, three minutes later, but placing fourth. She took a prize, however, for covering the course in the quickest time under the time allowance system, in the mixed class. The following day's race to Travemünde was also squally, cold and blowing hard. *Westward* got away well and after a thirty mile run rounded the mark first, holding her lead on the next reach of fourteen miles and the final twenty-nine mile close-reaching leg, beating *Germania* in by one minute, thirty-eight seconds boat for boat. Cochran wrote that it was the 'most interesting race yet and a great performance', and it resolved any argument about her performance in stronger winds. The prize was the Emperor's Cup.

Meteor IV *leading the older black-hulled* Hamburg (*ex* Rainbow) *downwind, and flying the Prussian eagle. Both have men aloft at spreaders or mastheads. (1909)*

# Chapter 3

While *Westward* is cruising down Channel bound back to Southampton, it might be a good time to outline the further unpleasantness that she was about to get herself enmeshed in, as soon as she arrived at Cowes.

British yachting in 1910 was, to put it bluntly, in a first class mess. The rules defining the measurement of yachts to obtain their rating (necessary in order to allow non-identical craft to compete against each other) were constantly being changed, usually for the worse, and yachting, like cricket, suffered from a surfeit of pundits. One well known yachting personality declared that the handicapping system had now become so complex that the only things that really knew who had won, were the yachts themselves; another cynic declared that it was rather like a children's party – if you stayed around long enough you were sure to get a prize. More seriously, unhealthy tendencies developed in yachts attempting to 'beat' the rule by maximizing speed-producing aspects of design while evading penalties in the rating formula. These created pressure for further change, which in turn made owners reluctant to order new boats or alterations to improve competitiveness.

As *Westward* made her way into the Solent, the handicapping committee was already at work deciding how to handicap the new Yankee schooner. They were in for a shock, for on requesting to come aboard and discuss the handicap, they were told firmly but politely that *Westward* would accept no handicap: she would only race in the A Class of the International Rule for which she had been designed, and under its time allowance scales. Mr Cochran was polite but firm, A Class or nothing, and the committee took a very dim view indeed. As he had spent a great deal of time and money to produce a perfect boat, if she was not to be given a fair chance in English waters he was quite prepared to return with her to America.

Meteor III *and* Germania *(A3) at Cowes*

*Charlie Barr in 1888 aboard* Shona *in Lawley's yard, South Boston, Massachusetts. A perfect example of a plank-on-edge cutter, a type encouraged by the British measurement rule of the period, she was 42 ft overall with a beam of 5 ft 8 in, and drew 6 ft 4 in. The Burgess-designed America's Cup defender* Volunteer *behind her typifies the contrasting form of American yachts.*

Despite the generally adverse press in England over the matter, Herbert L Reiach, wrote in *Yachting Monthly* in 1910: '*Westward* not sailing in handicap races has aroused considerable comment, but her refusal to start under their conditions can hardly be wondered at: she was designed and built to race in her class and under a fixed time allowance. People who spoke and wrote of her as a racing machine compared to the other boats, are seemingly unconscious of the fact that she conforms with the requirements of her class as to dimensions and construction. Her owner was well advised in not placing her at the mercy of the handicappers.'

Due to the firmness of Mr Cochran, who meant every word about taking *Westward* straight back to America, the schooner was eventually allowed to race under the A Class rules. In three Solent races she won decisively; this made a season's record of eleven firsts in eleven starts in open (i.e. non-handicap) races.

The Royal London Yacht Club race over a fifty-two mile course, on August 1, was *Westward*'s début in British yacht racing, and at Cowes.

| | rating (metres) | time allowance | finishing time | corrected time |
|---|---|---|---|---|
| *Westward* (Mr A S Cochran) | 29.09 | 6.56 | 2.58.52 | 2.51.56 |
| *Shamrock* (cutter) (Sir Thomas Lipton) | 23.00 | 9.32 | 3.13.12 | 3.3.40 |
| *Germania* (Herr Krupp Von Bohlen und Halbach) | 31.45 | scratch | 3.26.31 | 3.26.31 |
| *Meteor IV* (Kaiser Wilhelm II) | 31.522 | scratch | 3.31.59 | 3.31.59 |

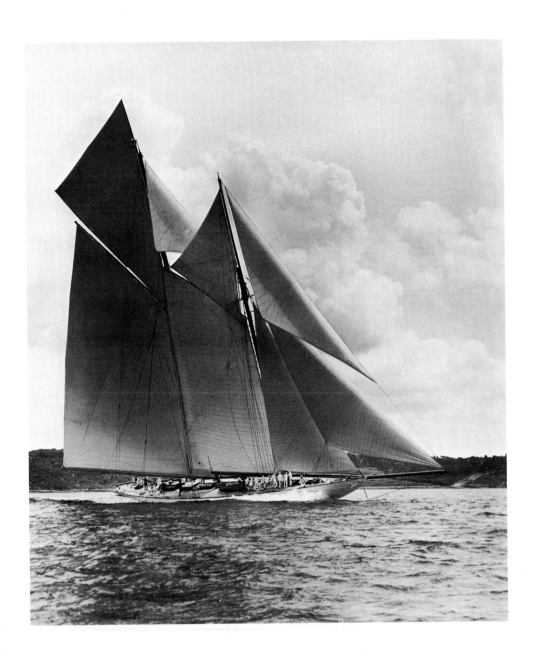

| | rating (metres) | time allowance | finishing time | corrected time |
|---|---|---|---|---|
| *Cicely* (Maj. C Whitaker) | 26.62 | 14.44 | 3.59.37 | 3.44.53 |
| *Susanne* (M. Verstraete) | 23.25 | 32.4 | 4.13.42 | 3.41.38 |

At the Nab lightship *Westward* led *Shamrock* by four minutes after a close reach and beat. The light southerly breeze then freshened, and the second time round was a dead beat to windward, *Shamrock* finishing second, fourteen minutes behind. While strictly speaking she should not have been racing in this class, her appearance provided more exciting competition and allowed comparison between a top 23 Metre cutter and *Westward*. (Because of Cochran's decision not to race in handicap events his schooner did not meet other Big Class yachts until after the war.)

The race on Wednesday, August 3 was conducted by the Royal Yacht Squadron for the Emperor's Cup; *Meteor IV* did not enter. The course was forty-seven miles, the old Queen's course, and there was a nice whole-sail breeze.

| | time allowance | finishing | corrected |
|---|---|---|---|
| *Westward* | 6 min 16 sec | 2.31.1 | 2.24.45 |
| *Germania* | scratch | 2.31.47 | 2.31.47 |
| *Cicely* | 13.19 | 2.41.48 | 2.28.29 |
| *Susanne* | 28.59 | 2.58.32 | 2.29.33 |

*Westward under her racing canvas, closehauled off the Isle of Wight in 1910, her first season*

By being over the line at the gun, *Westward* had to go back and lost three minutes.

Thursday's Squadron race for the Town prizes was to include the usual four schooners and *Julnar*, *Cariad II* and *Gertrude*. The Cochran scrapbook contains a card listing the handicaps, with *Westward* scratch (fastest) boat. She was to allow the others between fourteen and eighty-four minutes in light weather, and eleven to fifty-three minutes in rough weather: evidently her performance in the conditions found during the Week had impressed the handicappers. Unfortunately her owner did not expand upon his conversations with the local experts on what must have been an urgent matter; he noted that he lunched with some of the Sailing Committee at the Squadron, motored on the following day, and took a party of guests for a sail on Saturday.

*Westward*'s last race of the season was the opening race of Ryde Week, conducted by the Royal Victoria Yacht Club at Ryde, IOW on August 8, for a 600 guinea gold cup and a silver salver. The fifty-one mile course was shortened to one round because of the lack of wind.

| *Westward* | 6 min 48 sec | 4.41.40 |
| *Germania* | scratch | 6.42.53 |
| *Meteor IV* | scratch | 6.50.3 |
| *Cicely* | 14.27 | 6.57.30 |
| *Susanne* | 24.39 | retired |

After about seven hours' racing in a very light, fluky breeze, *Westward* finished two hours before the others.

*Captain Karpf of* Meteor *coming aboard* Westward *and being greeted by Captain Barr.*

While the schooner sailed across to Southampton, and her owner returned to the United States, it was reported, and never denied, that the Kaiser tried very hard, even through diplomatic channels, to get *Westward* to return to the Fatherland to make her permanent home in the Baltic.

Her season over, Barr prepared her for laying up in a mud berth at Summers & Payne in Southampton for the winter. She had completed a very successful year and Alexander Cochran had enjoyed every minute of it, except for the smoking incident, and

*Mr and Mrs Cornelius Vanderbilt, Mr R B Perkins, Major Heckstall-Smith and Captain Karpf, guests of A S Cochran for the Emperor's Cup race at Cowes, August 3, 1910. The Vanderbilt launch is alongside; Barr is taking their coats as Cochran takes the photo. The Emperor's yacht did not compete, and* Westward *won the cup after an exciting race.*

the attempts of those who were losing, to change the rules. Realizing that all this had been made possible by his family's thriving carpet manufacturing business, he sat down one evening and worked out exactly how much *Westward* had cost him to date, including his three months' vacation in Europe, which was a considerable sum even in 1910. He then made out a cheque for a similar amount to be distributed among all the hands at the carpet factory, thanking them for making it possible for him to have such a lovely boat; one has to admit that this was very advanced thinking for a New York industrialist sixty-five years ago.

Charlie Barr was at the zenith of his career as a racing skipper in 1910, with *Westward* tuned to perfection, and his great skill in keeping every inch of the schooner's huge reaching and running kites at work was something for all to wonder at. Those of us who have gybed round a racing mark in a stiff breeze, with other boats converging from different directions, should stop to think for a moment what that was like for the racing skippers of the day. *Westward* would be creaming along at anything up to fourteen knots, all 323 tons of her, and the skipper not only had to watch for other craft converging on the racing mark but had to keep his eye on the multiplicity of sails and rigging aloft; everything to be nursed through the gybe without carrying any of the gear away or getting snarled up. Racing skippers at that time were real professionals, and held in high regard by hands and yachtsmen alike; Barr was felt to be able to take his pick of racing yachts, and those who preferred not to credit *Westward* for her success could claim that it was in good part due to her skipper.

In yachting circles, the customary arguments continued after the season was over. To place in perspective

*Passing one of the Solent forts. Barr is at the helm and the crew are putting a jib in stops.*

back up to deck level; D was the difference between G and the 'skin' girth measured along the surface of the cross-section of the hull. Length, breadth or beam, sail area and freeboard also entered into the final calculation. Under the extant rule, a slight alteration in the measured hull dimensions would permit a large increase in the amount of sail carried without an unfavourable change in the rating figure. A yacht's rating was used, in conjunction with standard tables, to arrive at a time allowance for a given race, usually reckoned on the length of the course ('time on distance') rather than on the time taken ('time on time'). The advantage of this system was that competitors knew how they stood in relation to each other, and were not subject to sailing committees' fairness or favour. While it was a form of 'handicapping' in the ordinary sense of the word, there was another practice, whereby yachts which were not only different but possibly designed under various rules could race together with handicaps assigned to equalize their chances. This was not universally approved of, as improvement in design, sails or drill meant simply being handicapped further, and it was hardly incorruptible. (It was races of this sort in which Cochran had refused to enter *Westward*.) However, the weakness of successive rating rules had led to an unhealthy situation in British yachting, and for some time racing owners were reluctant to build when only 'rule-beaters' appeared to have a chance to win, and the result of successful loophole-seeking was eventual change in the rules, penalizing the offenders. The expense of building and altering yachts, particularly in the larger classes, made this unattractive (particularly after the rules changed against one), and by the time *Westward* was built there was a dearth of competition, with small

the concern expressed over *Westward*'s rating, it is necessary to point out that under the time allowance system used in racing in International Rule classes, the yachts' rating were the basis for balancing out their inequalities of size or other speed-enhancing elements. The hull and sail areas were measured at specified points, and the data inserted in the formula $\frac{1}{2}(L+B+\frac{1}{2}G+3D+\frac{1}{2}\sqrt{SA}-F)=$ rating. Briefly, G referred to 'chain girth' measured from deck level round the keel and entries in the bigger classes. (Hence, also, the frequently expressed hopes that she would give the Big Class a boost.) For reassurance, owners tended to go in for what were more or less cruisers built to Lloyd's scantlings, of no particular size or rating: while this avoided some of the excesses seen in the past, it failed to protect their investment, in that such boats did not fit any class well and were not every buyer's taste.

The following was published in 'Notes on Yachting' in *Yachting Monthly*, Vol. X, and while it only deals with an aspect of this picture, illustrates the sort of discussion which was current. It appeared under the title 'Is *Westward* Fairly Rated?'.

'There is a parenthetic clause in the rating rule which may presently prove confusing. In the "Instructions to Measurers", paragraph 17, the girth mark (G) is to be fixed at or abaft 0·55 from the fore end of the waterline. If the keel abaft that point is straight (except for a reasonable round up of the extreme after end) the greatest girth may exceed the girth at G by no more than 3 per cent. In all other cases the girth mark G must be fixed where the girth measurement is greatest. The clause was intended to allow a short turn at the sternpost heel. But what is a reasonable round up? If a certain latitude is allowed in, say, a 6 Metre boat, a proportional enlargement will be a considerable matter in a large schooner. It is also interesting to note in regard to this clause of the rules that there is no indication as to the direction in which the keel line must be straight. It may run up aft to the waterline, it may be level with the waterline, or it may drop, as is the case in nearly every instance.

'In small craft the draft is generally wanted, and the

Germania *close behind* Westward. *The crew are getting in the mainsheet, and she is harder on the wind: this may be the luffing incident at which* Germania *protested (not sustained).*

*Alex Cochran and guests enjoying the downwind leg of the race with the fleet left well behind.*

keel is dropped in a straight line to take advantage of the 3 per cent allowance, but where a big boat is concerned the draft may not be desired. Then the keel may run parallel to the waterline, or even rise slightly towards the stern of the boat. This brings me to a notable exception to the general practice – *Westward*. No authoritative statement has ever been made as to whether this yacht was designed under the International Rule; a careful study of her underwater profile suggest that she was not.

'She has a rocker keel, and one cannot conceive a designer of Herreshoff's ability throwing away the advantage obtained by some alteration in his lines. Apparently, however, his judgement in this matter— if, as I have said before, he considered it at all—does not appear to have been penalized. The girth marks seem to be at 0.55 of the waterline length from forward, and the keel being a rounded one, the measurement gives the 3 per cent allowance without the boat's having conformed to the requirements of such a case. Nor can this rocker keel be considered "a reasonable round up". One cannot imagine such elasticity of the clause being permitted.

'*Westward*'s greatest girth looks to be much further aft than her marks are placed, which would make some considerable difference in her rating. In past instances Herreshoff has made few mistakes in judging a rule, and it was the memory of this fact that suggested some advantage in the rocker keel. So far I have failed to find it, and if anyone can see profit in adopting such formation, the reason should be interesting. The extra draft available under our rule is not wanted in *Westward*'s case if it was designed under the American [Universal] Rule. Hence, most probably, the rocker keel.'

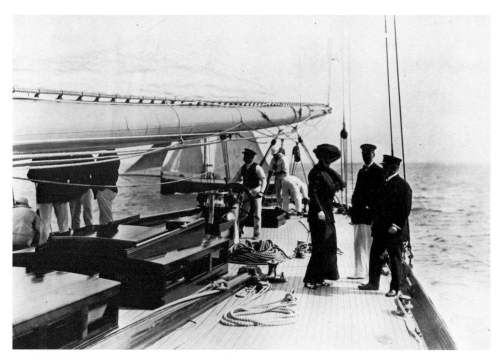

*After the race. The crew are tidying up, the main boom is sheeted in amidships and held there with extra tackles, the running backstays on both sides are set up, and the mainsail is about to be lowered. The small winch by the spinnaker boom behind Mrs Vanderbilt, is for jib topsail sheets.*

A reply by Herbert L Reiach appeared in *Yachting Monthly*.

'The paragraph which appeared in these pages last month on the subject of *Westward*'s measurement has aroused considerable interest; as it has also given rise to some misunderstanding, the situation may be briefly reviewed. At the outset I may say that no suspicion of unfairness attaches to *Westward*'s owner, designer or late Captain. The yacht was designed according to Herreshoff's idea of a fast schooner, and left to take her chance with our rule of measurement. According to the rules of the Yacht Racing Association the marks must be verified by the measurer; thus the yacht's representative had no say in the placing of them. Unfortunately, in *Westward*'s case the keel profile was overlooked, and the G marks fixed at 0.55 of the waterline length, measured from its fore end, instead of where the girth measurement was greatest. As I thought, the cambered keel was not considered a reasonable round up, but the yacht was measured as if having a keel which was straight abaft 0.55 of the water-line length, measured from its fore end. Thus the rounded keel went free of taxation. Fortunately, *Westward* won her races with sufficient time in hand to put disqualification out of the question, and her rating having been measured and given to her by the YRA, she is entirely without blame and could not have been disqualified in any case. But in all fairness to the English and German yachts which competed with her the corrected measurements should be published, as required by Clause XXII. Otherwise we have no line of comparison for reference, and if *Westward* goes to America without meeting Mr Whitaker's new yacht

[*Waterwitch*], we must remain in the dark as to the latter's qualities. As an alteration in the position of the girth measurement affects the factors G and D it will materially influence *Westward*'s margins, while not being sufficient to affect her successful record. Mr Cochran is, of course, at liberty to do as he likes with his yacht, more especially as he gave no undertaking to remain another season in British waters; but in the interest of sport it is to be hoped he will reconsider his plans and endeavour to keep *Westward* on this side in order to try conclusions with Mr Whitaker, who certainly deserves some reward for his enterprise. One could not wish for a better outlook than the racing such matches would provide.

'If the English schooner is doomed to go through the coming season without meeting a worthy antagonist her owner's disappointment will be shared by all who have the interests of yacht racing at heart.'

*Westward*'s future was far from certain. True, her owner was keen to race her against the latest Herreshoff schooner, Morton Plant's *Elena*, during the 1911 season, but during his visit to England he had consulted a specialist in London who had told him to take life more slowly. Also, the German Emperor was still determined to have *Westward* in the Baltic, and he was not accustomed to being refused.

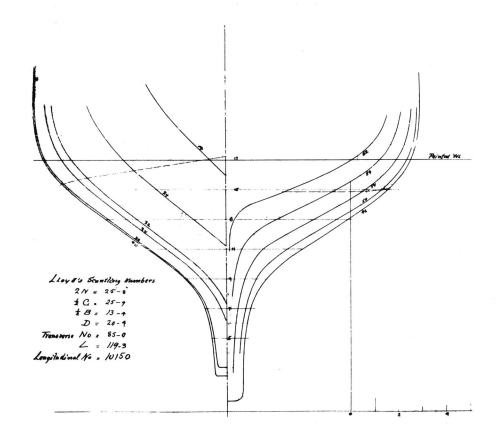

Lloyd's Scantling Numbers
$2N = 25-8$
$\frac{1}{2}C = 25-9$
$\frac{1}{2}B = 13-4$
$D = 20-4$
Transverse No = 85-0
$L = 119-3$
Longitudinal No = 10150

Painted WL

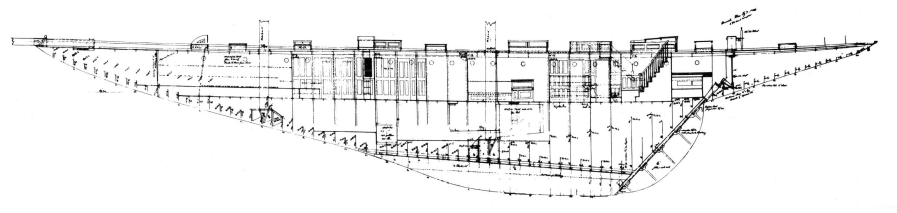

# Chapter 4

It is said that nothing succeeds like success: in the case of *Westward* this was unfortunately not true. No one realized it at the time, but she was already in a decline that was to last for nine long years.

In her first year, 1910, *Westward* had become universally known in yachting circles in Britain, the United States and on the Continent, and even attracted mention in the general press. It was only natural that great things were expected of her in the seasons that lay ahead. To suggest a few reasons for what went wrong may be unfair as the people concerned are no longer with us to state their views, but on the other hand I feel that we might be very near the truth.

On January 24, 1911 Captain Barr died very suddenly in Southampton. Alex Cochran was heartbroken on hearing of his death, for they had a very close bond in *Westward*, and he told his family that things would never be the same again aboard her now that Charlie had gone. One of the greatest racing skippers of all time, over the years Barr had been in charge of the famous racers *Ingomar*, *Minerva*, *Navahoe*, *Vigilant*, *Columbia* and *Reliance*, and took command of the big three-masted schooner *Atlantic* in the race for the Emperor's Cup, from Sandy Hook to the Lizard, when she made a passage of twelve days four hours, averaging ten and a half knots.

Such a man was difficult to follow, and not only did his death affect the morale of the crew, but they were held in suspense for a time while a new skipper was chosen. Several names had been mentioned in the press, but it was finally decided that Captain John (Chris) Christensen should take command; he had been mate under Charlie Barr in the past and was a very good and able seaman, but whether he had quite the same flair was another matter. It was also the case that *Westward* had been put up for sale after laying up at Summers & Payne in Southampton, for around $100,000 (then about £20,000). At the same time there was speculation in the American and British yachting press about possible competitors which might be commissioned,

Vanitie

and the usual hopes that she might stimulate a revival of schooner racing.

It was also reported that Alex Cochran was still far from well, and as he had been the main driving force behind the whole project, it was only natural that the pace should have slackened. His friends knew that despite the specialist's advice he was about to order two more yachts. They were to be designed by William Gardner and built by George Lawley & Son at Neponset, Massachusetts, the first to be ready for racing in 1914. She was *Vanitie* and designed as an America's Cup defender; her hull was made of steel and bronze, an advanced but fashionable material at that time. *Vanitie* never had to defend the America's Cup, for *Shamrock IV* heard the news of the outbreak of war when in Bermuda and sailed on to New York, where she was laid up until 1920. *Resolute* was chosen as the Cup defender after the war, and Cochran gave *Vanitie* to the New York Yacht Club; she was re-rigged as a schooner in 1925–6 and subsequently bought by Mr Gerald Lambert who restored her to sloop rig and sailed her until 1939.

The second of the two, the 230 foot *Sea Call*, was for cruising only. Built in 1915 in the United States to the design of William Gardner, this three-masted schooner has been called the finest sailing yacht in the world. She carried 18,000 square feet of canvas and cost nearly £100,000 yet within a few months of her launching she was broken up for scrap. The hull was apparently built of steel and monel metal (a copper-nickel alloy) and when she was drydocked after work-up and prior to her maiden voyage it was found that she was riddled with electrolysis of the most active nature. Nothing could be done to save this expensive ship, so she was scrapped after a life of only five months. The monel

Warrior. *She went on the rocks off Fisher's Island, off the Connecticut coast, in 1916.*

cost 42 cents a pound; the final figure of her cost was between $500,000 and $600,000. Reportedly, Cochran's friends in the legal profession advised him to sue the designers, but this he refused to do, on the grounds that if one experiments with untried metals, one must face up to disaster as well as success.

Alex Cochran was very pro-British, and as soon as war was declared he at once made a present of his large steam yacht *Warrior* to the Admiralty; he also ordered five fast motor torpedo boats to be built by Lawleys of Boston, and given to the Admiralty, which must have been some of the earliest PT-type boats used operationally by the Royal Navy. Cochran felt that they were excessively oriented towards battleships and cruisers, and failed to see the potential of high speed small craft: this advanced thinking was to be proved right in World War Two. The Admiralty, to show their appreciation, made him a commander in the Royal Naval Reserve, to continue as captain of *Warrior*.

This fabulously wealthy bachelor also ordered yet another three-masted schooner, *Vira*, 699 tons and of composite construction. She was designed by Charles E Nicholson and built by Camper & Nicholson at Gosport in 1927. On viewing her for the first time Cochran was so intimidated by the very size and power of the yacht, and then a very sick man, that he insisted on having all three masts lopped by fifteen feet, necessitating unstepping them and altering the rigging and sails. On a second visit he asked for a further fifteen feet to be taken off, thus ruining a beautiful boat. He died shortly afterwards and *Vira* was put on the market; her subsequent varied history is typical of many other schooners. She was bought by Major E W Pope, renamed *Creole*, and sailed regularly between Southampton and the Royal Yacht Squadron at Cowes, thus acquiring the nickname 'Pope's ferry'; then sold again to Sir Connor Guthrie who had her remasted and rerigged to Nicholson's original design. As *Magic Circle* she did mine depolarizing work during World War Two and afterwards was sold to a shipping company in Germany. Again *Creole*, she has been owned for many years by Mr Stavros Niarchos, the Greek shipowner, who again restored her rig after her gear was destroyed at Gosport in a bombing raid.

The main talking point in any American yacht club in 1911 was the trial of strength about to take place between *Westward* and Herreshoff's latest schooner *Elena*, built for Morton F Plant who had owned the successful schooner *Ingomar* and various other yachts. Except for the fact that *Elena* had a centreboard in her keel and *Westward* was a pure keel boat, they were very much alike as the following figures show: *Westward* 323 tons, steel, LOA hull 109.8, LWL 96.1, breadth 27.1, draft 16.9 feet; *Elena* 323 tons, steel, LOA hull 112, LWL 96, breadth 26.7, draft 17.6 feet. *Westward* had been designed in the light of the European International Rule which entailed a girth measurement, whereas *Elena* was intended for rating under the American Universal Rule, and the forward end of her keel lead was deeper and less rounded up and the maximum draft slightly greater.

Other schooners were on the Atlantic coast ready to put up a fight—*Karina, Atlantic, Enchantress, Irolita* and *Endymion*—but the real attention was on the Herreshoffs' latest creation. The main regatta in August turned out to be a great disappointment. The wind was light and fluky, and *Elena* did well in those conditions. To confuse the issue further, the schooners *Irolita*, better known as the *Queen* (222 tons, built by Herreshoff in 1906), and *Enchantress* won occasionally. Although *Westward* took the Astor Cup, the results generally were inconclusive. At the end of the series Cochran decided to call it a day, and she was laid up at City Island and subsequently put up for sale for $120,000 (about £24,000). The yachting press gasped at this audacity, for in 1911 one could buy a new 15 Metre, fully fitted out for racing, for around $15,000 (£3000). Today she looks cheap, for here was 323 tons of steel racing schooner in perfect

*Alexander Smith Cochran in the uniform of a commander in the Royal Navy, a commission which he accepted in January 1917.*

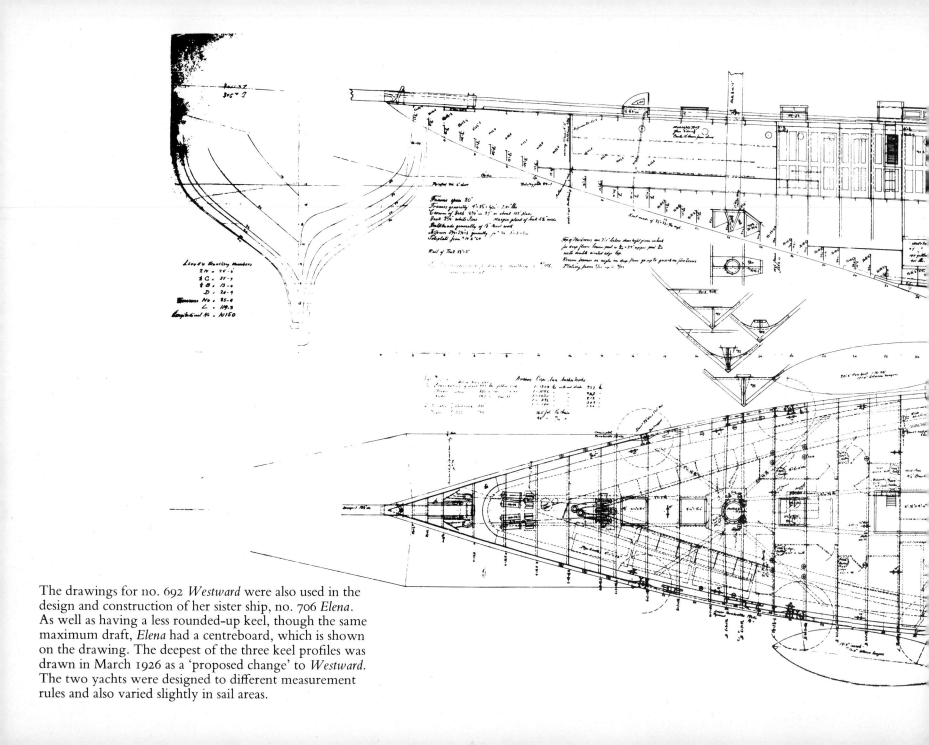

The drawings for no. 692 *Westward* were also used in the
design and construction of her sister ship, no. 706 *Elena*.
As well as having a less rounded-up keel, though the same
maximum draft, *Elena* had a centreboard, which is shown
on the drawing. The deepest of the three keel profiles was
drawn in March 1926 as a 'proposed change' to *Westward*.
The two yachts were designed to different measurement
rules and also varied slightly in sail areas.

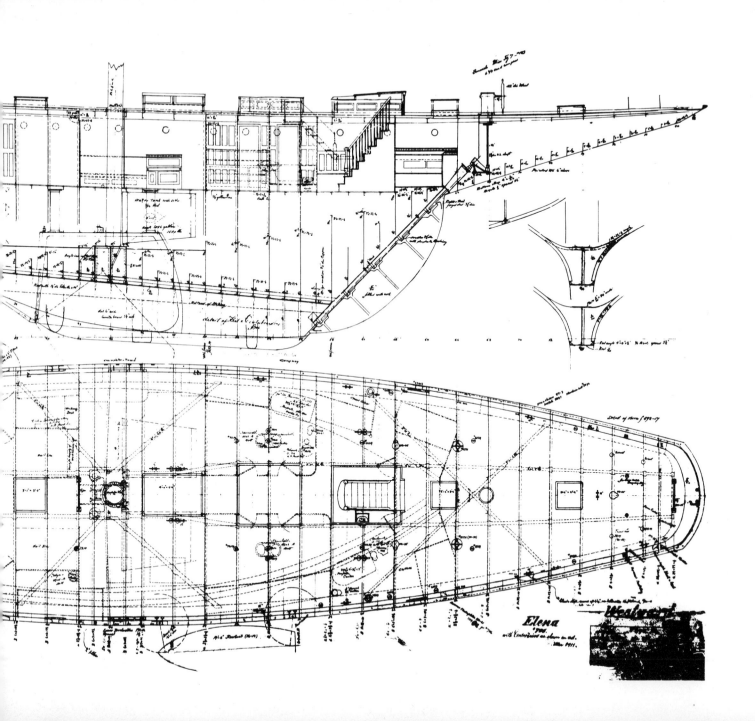

*Elena*

condition, with every chance of being in the prize money and yet capable of fast transatlantic passages, for the price of a very secondhand and well used modern ocean racer.

*Elena*, on the other hand, soon struck a winning streak, and became very successful in America, winning the Astor Cup in 1912, 1913 and 1916, and also the King's Cup and the Cape May Cup; in 1928 she won the large class in the transatlantic race to Santander, despite blowing out many of her sails.

Westward *on a reach, just after changing jib topsails. The main topmaststaysail set here is a deeper one that extends well below the foresail gaff. The other sails visible are, from forward, the jib topsail, jib and forestaysail; gaff foresail (with a jib-headed foretopsail set above it); and on the mainmast the main and maintopsail, here in the form of a jackyard topsail set on spars to extend beyond the topmast and gaff. The foot of the racing foresail is longer than the boom for improved airflow, and has to be taken round the mainmast when tacking (1910).*

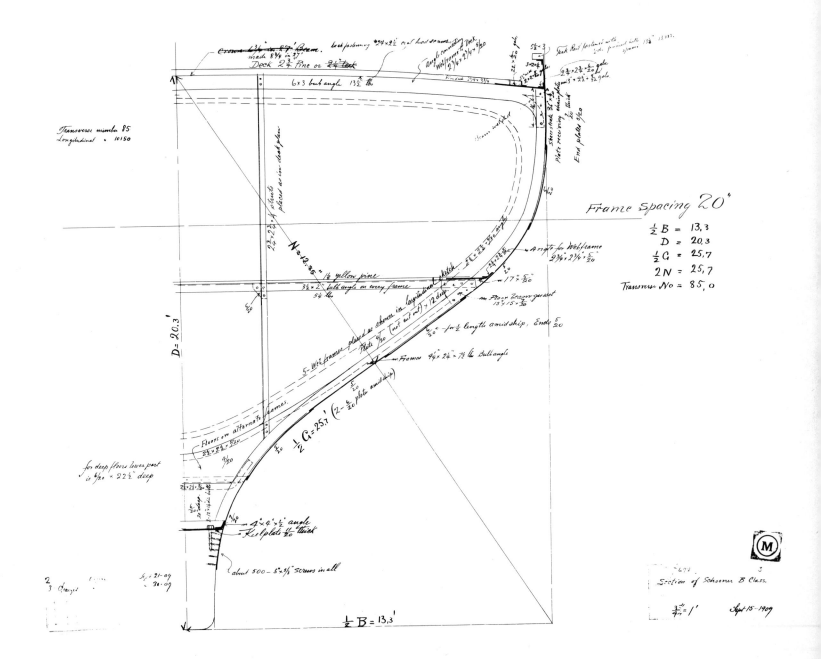

Crown 13/4" 27' Beam.
made 8 3/8 in 27'
Deck 2 1/4" Pine or 2 1/8" teak

Deck fastening #24 x 2 1/2" oval head screws

angle connecting Deck
Webframe 2 3/4 x 5/20
2 3/4 x 2 1/4 x 3 3/4

Tech Rail fastened with
sch. gunmetal bolts 13/8" 13.123.
spaces

6 x 3 bulb angle 13 1/2 lbs

5 1/2 x 3
3 x 2 1/4
22 x 2 0 gals.

2 3/4 x 2 1/4 x 20 gals.
13 x 2 1/2 x 1/2 gals.

Sheer strak 3 1/2 x 1/4
Plate receiving thimbles
20 thick
End plate 5/20

Transverse number 85
Longitudinal " 10150

Frame Spacing 20"

1/2 B = 13,3
D = 20,3
1/2 G = 25,7
2 N = 25,7
Transverse No = 85,0

N = 12.85   1/2 yellow pine

3 1/2 x 2" bulb angle on every frame
5 1/2 lbs

Angle for Webframe
2 3/4 x 2 1/4 x 5/20

17" x 5/20

Floor Beam gusset
15 x 15 x 5/20

2 3/4 x 2 1/4 x 5/8 angle

for 1/2 length amidship, Ends 5/20

5- Web frames placed as shown in longitudinal sketch
Plate 4/20 (not cut out) x 12 deep

Frames 4 1/2 x 2 1/4 x 7 1/2 lb Bulb angle

Floors on alternate frames.
2 1/4 x 2 1/4 x 5/20
5/20

D = 20.3

1/2 G = 25,7 (2 - 6/20 plate amidship)

for deep floors lower part
is 6/20 x 22 1/2" deep

2 1/4 x 2 1/4 x 3/4
20 deep
2 1/2 x 4 1/2 bolt

4 x 4 x 1/2" angle
Keel plate 11/20 thick

about 500 - 5 x 3/8" screws in all

2 Changes
3 Changes

Sept 21-09
30-09

Section of Schooner B Class.

3/4" = 1'     Sept 15-1909

1/2 B = 13,3'

# Chapter 5

For Kaiser Wilhelm II of Germany it was true that 'everything comes to those who wait', for in October 1912 *Westward* sailed for the Baltic to become part of the German fleet of steel schooners. She had been purchased by a syndicate in the name of the Norddeutschen Regatta Verein, Seefahrt, Hamburg, and the General Director of the Hamburg-American line, Albert Ballin, made himself responsible for her third voyage across the Atlantic. On arrival she was slipped, her beautiful white hull painted jet black, the name *Westward* was painted out, and emblazoned across her stern was *Hamburg II*. Unfortunately, her new owners altered the sail plan, adding another 3489 square feet of canvas; they also put in a lot of unnecessary weight in the form of extra cabin furniture as well as a piano, which seemed a very strange thing to do to a racing yacht, and she also acquired a German crew.

The Kiel Regatta of 1913 was dominated by the new British A Class racing schooner *Margherita*, a beautiful boat designed and built by Charles E Nicholson for Major Cecil Whitaker. She returned from Kiel with five first prizes: a splendid performance. On the race to Laboe from Kiel on June 27 the result was *Margherita* first, *Meteor IV* second, *Hamburg II* third and *Germania* last. The German Emperor, The Prince of Monaco and Admiral von Tirpitz, Secretary to the Navy, were on board *Meteor*. *Margherita* had a time allowance of one minute, eight seconds from *Meteor IV* and *Germania*, and *Hamburg II* had an allowance of four minutes, thirty-two seconds. The return race from Kiel to Eckernförde on July 2 was won by *Margherita* with *Hamburg II* second, and in the July 3 race from Kiel to Travemünde *Meteor* was first followed by *Hamburg II*. Apart from these few successes her performance was mediocre, and she was placed below *Germania* when the final results were declared (in 1910 she had proved faster than *Germania*). After the Kiel Regatta *Hamburg II* was laid up, some say in disgrace, leaving *Meteor* and *Germania* to represent the German schooners at Cowes.

The non-arrival of *Hamburg II* in British waters for

the 1913 season was a deep disappointment, for her performance in home waters against *Margherita*, and the older competition which she had so decisively beaten in 1910, was of wide interest. Schooner racing in Europe and Britain was past its heyday and largely sustained by the Germans, a few older British yachts, and American designs built to the Universal Rule. In Big Class racing generally, it was felt that top competition was needed to reward and justify the effort and expense of building new yachts of this size; once *Westward* had proved her quality, there was more stimulus to commission new schooners. *Elena* in the United States and *Waterwitch* in Britain were naturally designed in hopes of beating her, and their matches widely reported. William Fife had been given the job of providing Whitaker with a suitable replacement for his *Cicely*, and produced *Waterwitch*, which had only the Germans to face in 1911 as *Westward* had returned to the United States. She was well beaten, and modification did not improve her results in 1912. *Margherita* was built the following winter, and Nicholson's design was considerably more gratifying to her owner. She was slightly larger than *Westward* and carried more sail, and her excellence was shown by her triumph at Kiel over a fleet which had benefited from alteration and lightening, and at Cowes. The yachting press, who had been sharpening their pencils to report on a needle match, were very disappointed and contented themselves with making adverse remarks about *Hamburg II* sulking in the Baltic.

For some reason, she did not receive a good press in Europe. From Germany, still smarting under their 1910 defeats, one correspondent wrote: 'Last year we were badly bluffed by the matchless *Westward* under the able command of the late Charles Barr. It was not until

*Kaiser Wilhelm II (1859–1941), who wanted* Westward

too late that this boat was found to be a mere racing machine and even her measurements wrong.' Several of the yachting pundits in Britain, who should have known better, referred to her as 'that racing machine'; this one finds hard to understand, for of course she was a racer, which was the object of the exercise, but on the other hand she had been proved a very good sea boat: what more could one ask of any designer?

The 'racing machine' myth was finally laid to rest once and for all by Charles E Nicholson himself, in an open letter to *Yachting Monthly*.

'Americans need no better proof of the value of sound construction than the beautifully modelled American schooner *Westward*, which Mr A S Cochran insisted should be built to Lloyd's highest class. She crossed the Atlantic three times with her racing masts; she has raced here, on the Continent and in America, and she is still as sound as when new. Contrast her with the Cup challengers and defenders of the past thirty years. They were useless for any other purpose than that for which they were designed, and soon became mere "junk".'

In 1914 war clouds were gathering fast and Winston Churchill was busy mobilizing the Grand Fleet. *Hamburg II* and *Meteor IV* stayed in the Baltic and raced in the Kiel Regatta, but the big yachts did not finish the race which took place on June 28, when the news was passed to them of the murder of the Austrian successor to the throne and his wife, in Sarajeivo. War was declared during Cowes Week, and people were saying 'this is the end of yachting on the grand scale', but once again the popular experts were wrong.

Meteor IV. *Her stemhead ornamentation is very distinctive. Two crew are on the forward spreaders handling the spinnaker boom, which rests in a fitting on the forward side of the mast.*

# Chapter 6

Nineteen hundred and nineteen was the year of reassessment. The Kaiser, now deprived of his schooners, was in exile; 9,700,000 people had lost their lives; a generation of young men had virtually been wiped out; and 15,000,000 tons of shipping lay rotting on the ocean bed. Those of us who survived, after four years' malnutrition were facing the worst influenza epidemic in living memory, sweeping through Europe, America and Asia like a prairie fire. But such is the resilience of the human race that within a year we were entering a period known as the 'swinging twenties', and what is more, even thinking about yacht racing once again. Boat builders, who had been geared to war production for so long, were busy looking for the blueprints of the yachts that they had been about to build in 1914, as well as trying to repair the ravages of four years of neglect on boats either laid up or used by the Services during hostilities. Of all those who were engaged in re-establishing yacht racing, the main credit in Britain must surely go to King George V himself, for he gave instructions for

*Britannia* to be removed from her mud berth in the Medina River at Cowes where she had lain for four and a half years, and to be refitted ready for the 1920 racing season. This gesture by His Majesty was exactly what was necessary to put British yachting back on its feet once again, and it certainly affected the future of the big yachts that had been languishing ashore for so long.

*Hamburg II* in fact survived the war very well; she had been carefully laid up in the Kiel Canal with the rest of the German schooners, and as she had been built to the highest standards of materials and construction was still in excellent condition. Her new owner was Mr Clarence Hatry, a well known London financier, and the first thing he did after buying her as a war prize was to re-register her as *Westward*: her unhappy period as *Hamburg II* was soon forgotten. He also had the sail area reduced to 13,455 square feet.

As he was comparatively new to yacht racing as well as to *Westward*, it was only natural that he wanted to gain the necessary experience before taking on all comers, particularly in strong winds. In 1920 she was fitted out in the West Channel at Brightlingsea, Essex, under Captain Edward Sycamore who was her skipper for a short period. He had begun his racing career in the old 40 tonner *Foxhound*, followed in 1874 by the famous *Bloodhound*; he then worked for Admiral the Hon. Victor Montagu in the 40-Raters *Corsair*, *Vendetta* and *Carina*. In 1895 he was helmsman on the America's Cup challenger *Valkyrie III* for the Earl of Dunraven, and later still commanded *Shamrock II*, *Namara* and *Mariquita*. Much confusion generally on the question of skippers has been caused by the fact that they have been known to change yachts to act as 'guest skipper' where their local knowledge of wind and tides could be an advantage; in the case of *Westward*, Captain Harry Cross, previously on *Moonbeam*, had raced her on the Clyde and also in Belfast Lough.

As *Westward* missed the Clyde Fortnight in 1920, her first meeting with *Britannia* was at the Deal Regatta in July. Five boats came to the starting line, and although *Westward* was very fast downwind in the stiff breeze, *Britannia* was better closehauled; *Westward* had to give her twelve minutes, forty seconds on handicap and the royal cutter stormed across the finishing line at well over twelve knots, to win on her time allowance. The 23 Metre cutter *White Heather* was third; the schooner *Susanne* and Lord Sackville's *Sumurun* had retired in the rising wind. The following day the weather was so bad that Mr Hatry decided to stay at anchor, which as it turned out was a wise decision for the Solent Fortnight was only eleven days away and he did not want to do any damage to his boat. *Britannia* with reduced sail went down to the starting line, followed by Sir C Allom

*Clarence Hatry and his family sailing on* Westward *at Cowes.*

in *White Heather* while *Susanne* and *Sumurun*, like *Westward*, stayed out of the fray. The result of this race was expensive: *Britannia*'s steel boom collapsed (it had been dented by gybing against a jammed running backstay in a hard wind in a Clyde race); *White Heather*'s extremely expensive Marconi mast disintegrated and fell over the side, ruining the mainsail in the process, and ending a 'sail-over'.

The Cowes Regatta was memorable not only for the fact that most of the big yachts were back, but because the new Second International Rule for measurement and changes in the calculation of time allowances seemed an improvement over the pre-war state of affairs. The restriction placed on sail area had the effect of limiting manpower and cost, as well as encouraging more sensibly canvassed designs.

The Big Class racing fleet now consisted of *Britannia* (HM King George V) 221 tons, *Westward* (Mr Clarence Hatry) 323 tons, *Susanne* (Mr Warwick Brookes) 154 tons, *White Heather* (Sir Charles Allom) 151 tons, the ex-23 Metre *Nyria* (Mrs Workman) 169 tons, *Sumurun* (Lord Sackville) 92 tons, *Zinita* (Mr Lionel de Rothschild) 92 tons, the newly built cutter *Terpsichore* (Mr R H Lee) 175 tons, and also the 19 Metres *Narada* and *Corona*. *Westward*'s return to Cowes was very

*Westward running through Cowes Roads in 1920, the first season of Big Class racing after the war. She was then owned by Clarence Hatry. The adoption of a new rating rule provided much-needed encouragement to British yachting generally, and the King's decision to fit out* Britannia *gave a magnificent lead to first-class racing. The black-hulled steam yacht with twin funnels is the royal yacht* Victoria & Albert, *on which George V and Queen Mary stayed during Cowes week.*

different from her last appearance ten years before, when she had swept all before her. The press described her performance as disappointing, but given a good breeze she could still do well, and had a good fight in the first race on August 2 against *Britannia* sailed by the King, who beat *Westward* home by one minute, fifteen seconds; it was one of *Britannia*'s greatest races that year, and ranked with her famous victories over the American yachts *Navahoe* and *Vigilant* in past years.

At the end of the short season in 1920 *Westward* had only raced six times and won three prizes, none of which were firsts, so as far as Mr Hatry was concerned it had been a very expensive introduction to Big Class yachting. Her racing career was once more in jeopardy for her harassed owner had other things to think about besides yachting, and during the next four seasons she languished, either shored up in shipyards or lying in a mud berth up the Itchen River near Southampton.

There is little that one has to say about *Westward*'s third owner disappearing from the yachting scene. Clarence Charles Hatry was very unlucky: he had a vast financial empire with many brands in the fire, some of which were rather hot. During the postwar slump in 1920, Hatry had of his own volition made available the bulk of his private fortune (which at the time extended to £1,500,000) for the benefit of those of his companies adversely affected, or for the purpose of repurchasing shares which had temporarily depreciated. His active career in the City extended over a period of twenty years, but even he, despite all his experience, could not ward off the approaching catastrophe, and the Hatry Group was the first company in Britain to 'crash' after the tightening-up of money six months previously. For the same reason many people who could least afford

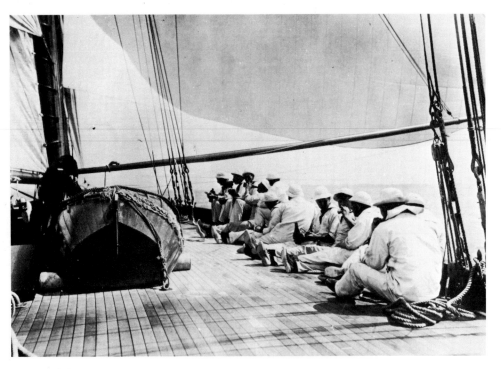

*Lunch while racing*

and as a result of their pressure on the Home Office his term in prison was reduced by eighteen months. It is said that if the Fraud Squad had held off for another forty-eight hours he would have been 'home and dry'. Whether this is true I do not know, but I am certain that he was not the avaricious villain that the popular press made him out to be.

Unravelling the story of a schooner after a lapse of fifty years is never easy, and here the picture becomes clouded, as the name of Mr Warwick Brookes of 12 Suffolk Street, Pall Mall, London appears as the owner of *Westward* in the 1924 edition of *Lloyd's Register of Yachts*. Mr Brookes was reputed to be a very keen yachtsman who had made his name racing 6 Metres on the Crouch; he then turned his attention to larger boats and purchased that very pretty Fife schooner *Susanne*, rescuing her from a dreary fate as a houseboat, and had her fully restored for the 1920 racing season.

It has been reported that the fitting out of *Susanne* and *Westward* was entrusted to Stone's Yard at Brightlingsea, and that they had been shored up side by side in front of the yard. Unfortunately, according to James & Stone, as the firm is now called, no records have been kept from as far back as the 1920s. However, I should imagine that to get a schooner of the size and draft of *Westward* ashore must have been no easy task even on spring tides.

The news that Mr Warwick Brookes had bought *Westward* was received with much satisfaction by yachtsmen all over the country, as it opened up the possibilities of a revival of a schooner class, but their hopes were not to materialize, and as far as I can ascertain her new owner never took her racing.

it were left virtually destitute, and the Wall Street crash occurred the following month in 1929.

For his part in this affair, Clarence Hatry was charged with fraud and forgery and sent to Maidstone Prison for fourteen years; many influential people, including Members of Parliament, considered this sentence savage,

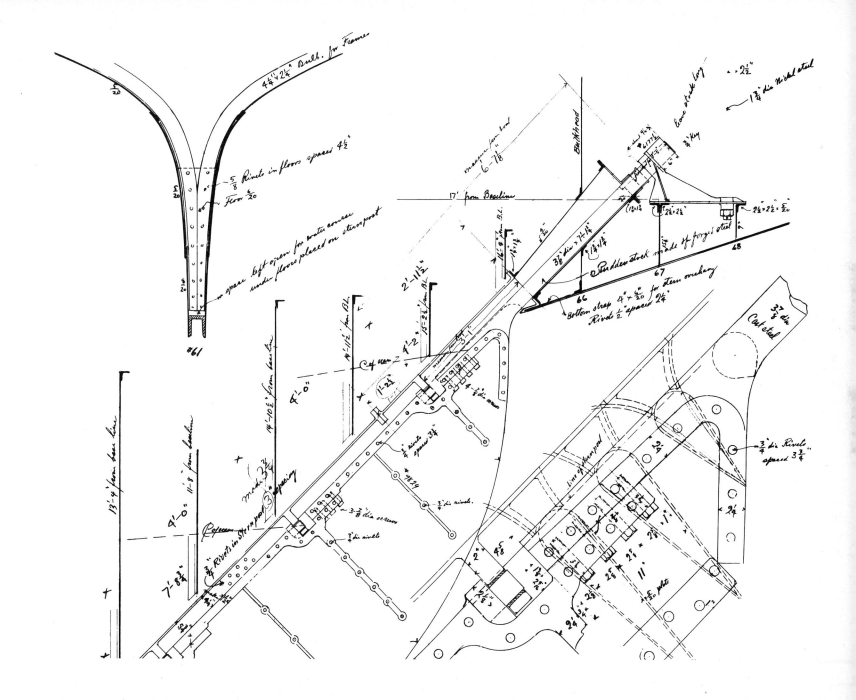

# Chapter 7

Although this is the story of *Westward*, she must be put in the background while I devote some time to a fantastic character who was about to become her last and most devoted owner: to be perfectly honest, it would be far easier to write a book about this astonishing man than about *Westward* herself, though I suppose they are synonymous.

Thomas Benjamin Davis, the son of a fisherman, was born at Havre-des-Pas, Jersey, Channel Isles in 1868. From the very beginning the sea was in his blood, for he grew up among boats of every type, and many hours when not at school were spent fishing around that rock-strewn coast. In 1883, at the age of fifteen, he signed on for his first deep water voyage away from the Channel Isles aboard the schooner *Satelite*, owned by Mr George Allix. During a northeasterly gale the ship struck the Haisborough Sands off the Norfolk coast twelve miles east of Cromer, and in the high seas the ship started to pound badly. The *Satelite*'s master, fearing that he might have to abandon her, put the longboat over the side on a long painter, with young Davis in it to receive the captain's logbook and personal effects, should the ship start to break up. One sea much larger than the rest burst over the schooner and the painter of the longboat parted under the strain. Davis and the boat were swept away across the shallows to disappear among the flying spindrift; the *Satelite* drove on the rising tide right across the sands and back into deeper water, and finally fetched up at Great Yarmouth, where a telegram was sent to Jersey, reporting young Davis missing and feared drowned.

After being adrift for nineteen hours, and half frozen with cold, he was rescued by the Norwegian trading schooner *Urda* of Stavanger, bound from Berga to Southampton with a cargo of oats. Eventually he returned to Jersey in the packet boat *Diana*, little worse for his adventures; and as he said in after life, 'It's not given to everybody to read his own obituary.' He lived for another sixty years.

Quite undaunted by this early experience, he made

the sea his career, and worked so hard at his chosen profession that at the age of twenty-five he received his Extra Master's ticket in 1892, one of the youngest seamen ever to have passed this exacting examination. From 1896 to 1899 he served in the Royal Naval Reserve. Shortly afterwards he gave up the sea and went to South Africa, where he started a really efficient stevedoring business, for he understood ships and how to load them, and more important still, how to handle native labour by giving them firm but fair treatment. His head office was in Durban, and I understand that he had other interests in Mozambique, East Africa and Angola. After making a fortune in Africa he returned to Jersey and settled down in a beautiful house over-looking St Brelade's Bay, and over the years became a great benefactor to the Island.

In 1933, when in Norway with *Westward* on the occasion of the centenary of yacht racing, T B Davis with the assistance of King Haakon sought out the only surviving member of the *Urda*'s crew, the ship's carpenter and the man who had actually pulled him out of the flooded longboat fifty years before. Not only did he reward him, but all the dependents of the other members of the crew, now long dead.

So here we have a man whose name is still well known among the older generation of yachtsmen, surrounded by stories, most of which have grown over the years and are no doubt exaggerated in the telling. Some might say that he was an extrovert, which in fact he was not: he was just himself, a prime seaman with a liking for calling a spade a bloody shovel, and one who under his gruff exterior could be kindness itself.

As far as the big racing class was concerned, costs were rising all the time and to maintain a large racing

*T B (hand on wheel) with his sailing master Alf Diaper (behind binnacle).*

manufacturer, an ex-stevedore, a brewer, an aeroplane maker, a house decorator, a newspaper proprietor and several shopkeepers. For some extraordinary reason, purveyors of alcohol were eventually deemed respectable and allowed to join the Squadron.

Of all those mentioned in the previous paragraph, the two men who had most in common, strange to relate, were the King and the ex-stevedore, T B Davis, for they were both professional seamen, one trained in the Royal Navy, the other in trading schooners. T B was on occasions quite capable of showing his crew how things were done, even to shinning up the masts without the aid of a bosun's chair, despite the fact that he was over fifty years old. This achievement together with his flow of language when things went wrong was held in the highest esteem by all the deckhands in the racing fleet. Not only did George V admire his ability to handle *Westward*, but once paid him the compliment of asking him to come aboard *Britannia* to advise on some obscure technical problem with the rigging, which Davis was able to solve; the King then turned to T B and told him, 'I always say you are the only sailor in the fleet.'

It had always been the practice in the big yachts to pay off the professional crew of sailing master, mates and hands at the end of the racing season. Whether they were re-employed in the following season depended solely on their past performance. Many of them came from the East Coast, where they spent the winter either fishing or working on the land. The yachts themselves were laid up with some reputable boatyard with instructions to spend the next six months working through the defects list, which after the rough and tumble of a full racing season could be quite extensive. By contrast,

yacht in peak of condition one had to be very rich indeed; the only people who could afford this constant outlay were those engaged in financially profitable pursuits. To be 'in trade' and not in a profession was definitely frowned upon, particularly by the Royal Yacht Squadron, who persistently refused entry to the club to anyone in that category; and it was ironical that in the big racing class, except for His Majesty's *Britannia*, the big yachts belonged to a sewing machine

T B Davis kept his whole crew, who were mainly Channel Islanders, in full employment all the year round, and except for his original visit to Camper & Nicholsons at Gosport in 1924 after purchasing *Westward*, and a few contacts with White's Shipyard on the River Itchen, all work was carried out by himself and his crew. The boat builders, shipyards and sailmakers were not going to make much money out of him.

The man chosen to be sailing master was Alf Diaper of Itchen, a most experienced seaman and a great character in his own right. He had made his name as skipper in Sir Charles Allom's 15 Metre cutter *Istria*, which was the first yacht in Britain to use the Marconi rig. As is so often the case, with two strong personalities in a small space the sparks used to fly. I don't know how many times Alf Diaper had threatened to resign during their long association, particularly as Alf enjoyed his drink and T B hardly if ever touched alcohol, therefore making reconciliations over a noggin difficult, but each of them had a great respect for the other's ability. They also had in common a very deep love for the schooner *Westward*, and despite the many scenes and upheavals over the years they stayed together to the end of her racing days.

Davis's approach to racing was different from everybody else's: he was a professional seaman himself, with little use for yacht hands as such, so his crew with very few exceptions were also deep water men. *Westward*'s working complement consisted of nineteen able seamen, a sailmaker and sailmaker's mate, a carpenter, engineer, first and second mates, the sailing master and Davis himself as captain; add to this a cook and two stewards and the owner's Rolls Royce trained chauffeur who also lived in the forecastle when the schooner was in

*His Majesty King George V sailing* Britannia. *When the royal yacht was scuttled after the King's death, his friend T B Davis pulled down* Westward's *racing flag.*

*Britannia in the early 1920s, rigged very similarly to G L Watson's original 1893 design with three headsails, jackyard topsail and separate topmast.*

port, and thirty-one people were involved. It was not unusual for Mrs Davis, who did not really like sailing, to be aboard, often accompanied by one of her two daughters. When racing at Cowes or Dartmouth, HM ships or yacht clubs would be asked to provide some extra hands, who usually found the experience of sailing with Davis memorable and subsequently added to the yarns about him. In the 1930s John Illingworth crewed on *Westward*, then the biggest yacht racing in Britain, in a handicap race against the big cutters *White Heather*, *Britannia* and *Nyria*, and later wrote the following:

'When we got back to the mooring he strode round the deck looking for jobs that ought to be done, and tossed me a sheet end—"Here, boy, put a whipping on that." Having once been a seaman himself in the Merchant Navy, I fancy he rather enjoyed addressing moderately experienced Naval officers in that way. Anyway, I quickly put an extremely strong whipping on the end of the headsail sheet, really pulling it home until it bit into the palm of my hand: I had heard about this trick of T B's. He came along a moment or two later and put his horny great thumbnail on it, thinking to rip off a poor whipping, instead of which he tore his thumbnail and departed with a priceless flow of language.'

The ship was run with a firm hand, under rules and traditions that were half naval and half mercantile marine. Able seamen wore dark blue serge trousers with blue jersey sweaters, with the name *Westward* across the chest in red, and also wore naval type caps with white covers for summer wear. They were inspected before going ashore, like a naval liberty party. The crew were not allowed to smoke abaft the foremast, and when at anchor, should they return from ashore after 10 p.m. they were not allowed to use the gangway but had to come inboard via the bobstay and bowsprit—no easy matter after a lot of beer. There was an extra five shillings per week good conduct money, but this was only paid at the end of the season, and one slip lost you the lot: if you enjoyed kicking over the traces, it paid to start at the beginning of the season.

Although T B was a non-smoker and also teetotal he loved parties, some of which went on into the small hours, but he always showed consideration for his personal steward by paying him one pound for every hour he kept him up after midnight. He did not approve of drinking while racing, and as some of his guests were very used to having a gin as soon as the sun was over the yardarm, a bottle was secreted on race days in the forecastle for the benefit of the hard-working male guests, who pretended to go down to use the forward heads. Whether T B ever found out I don't know, but if he did he closed his eyes to it. He also only tolerated women (other than family) on board and hated lipstick and females who wore trousers, and a skirt was kept in the loan clothing locker for just this eventuality.

Much has been said about his spectacular language, and this is something that has not been exaggerated over the years. During one of the Clyde Regattas *Westward* developed trouble with her rudder. T B found out that the Kilmun Pier in Holy Loch was not in use on Sundays, so he hired it for the day for *Westward* to lean against while repairs to the rudder were being made: near the pier was a church and after the service the congregation wandered down to admire the beautiful schooner. Suddenly from under the counter came the usual Davis fusillade, from which the local population and their children fled in disorder. The pastor of the church wrote to the owners of the pier that in future they must not hire it to Mr Davis, for his language had polluted his flock: to swear was bad enough, but on Sundays was quite unforgivable.

# Chapter 8

Before talking about racing, for after all that was what *Westward* was built for, a walk round the deck may be of interest for anybody who has never been near a sailing yacht of this size. The huge Oregon pine bowsprit dominated the foredeck. Many a competitor has quailed at the sight of its thrusting approach at high speed in a close-fought start, but due to her underwater sections and perfect sail balance she handled like a 6 Metre, and many a time it slid past the counter of another yacht with only feet to spare.

On the port and starboard side of the bow were heavy stocked anchors of the fisherman type. T B had used this type of anchor all his life; he had never been shipmates with the more modern equipment that was coming on the market and therefore did not trust it, any more than he trusted mooring buoys—'You never know what the links are like near the sinker,' he used to remark. He anchored every time. Anchoring *Westward* was easy enough, but getting it up again was quite another matter: the capstan was of the old pump type and it took four crew, two to each handle, to operate it; when you ran out of breath, for T B always put out that extra bit of chain, you changed places with the two men washing the links as they came inboard. The $1\frac{1}{4}$ inch chain had been specially forged for *Westward* after Davis bought her; part of it had been tested to destruction, and it was much stronger than the usual chain provided by ships' chandlers. Six people to get up the anchor, one would have thought, would have been enough, but two more hands down in the forecastle having taken up the centre floorboards would be leading the heavy chain aft from the spurling pipe and flaking it down at the foot of the foremast, so that the schooner did not become heavy by the head, upsetting her sailing trim.

Walking round the decks, one at once noticed how clear of obstructions they were. Any blocks which were made of brass were removed when not at sea, and their fixing points covered with brass plates; there were no winches worthy of the name though a few vestigial

*Urda*, and the schooner's only auxiliary power. When an engine was required, this boat was dropped into the water and lashed under the long counter, harnessed rather like a pony in a trap, only pushing rather than pulling.

A quick look at the interior might also be of interest. From the main companionway steps under the doghouse a passageway led forward to the saloon; on the port side were two cabins and a bathroom, to starboard a

*The tackle is for the running backstay to the mainmast head. Stanchions and lifelines were fitted for the Atlantic crossings, subsequently removed, but later replaced. (1910)*

specimens can be seen in the photographs. All halyards lead to the foot of the masts, and the absence of pulpit or stanchions helped to give the flush deck an appearance of great spaciousness; lifelines were rigged when necessary. The uncluttered sheerline was matched by low bulwarks capped with a teak rail. Deck planking was $2\frac{3}{4}$ inch pine over the steel plating.

Held in davits on the port side was a fast motorboat, and astern of it and also in davits a trim rowing dinghy. On the starboard side she carried a robust harbour launch, a 'maid of all work' named significantly

*Cracking along under lower canvas with the jib topsail stowed on the bowsprit and other sails on deck. The crew are up to weather, except for a man in the bows (possibly Davis). The anchor chains, spurling pipes and windlass can be seen on the foredeck. Stanchions and lifelines have been added to the bulwarks amidships. The weight of the wind is enough to bend the bowsprit sideways and its lee shrouds have slackened. (1930)*

*The cabinet holding two of Westward's cups was made by T B Davis. The two chests were on board: the smaller one contained cutlery and the larger, glasses and decanters. The upper trophy is the Messer Cup, a silver cup marking His Majesty's Jubilee and the 160th year of the Royal Thames Yacht Club, presented by Allen E Messer to 'the winner of the race around the Isle of Wight for schooner yachts exceeding 100 tons Thames measurement'. The other is the gold centenary King's Cup, presented by George V at the Royal Yacht Squadron Regatta in 1934. (The first King's Cup was presented to the Squadron by William IV in 1834.) These items form part of the Davis collection of the Société Jersaise in St Helier in the Channel Islands.*

chart space followed by the owner's cabin which was much larger than the others, with bathroom attached. A double cabin aft of the companionway extended across the width of the hull. The saloon also ran right across the ship, with the mainmast passing through the deckhead at the forward end of the compartment. This splendid spar had been looked after with loving care for fifteen years until it had matured to the colour of dark sherry. A photograph showed Mr Davis' daughter Marjorie at the wheel: she was reported to be a good helmswoman and was on occasions allowed the helm even when racing. The decor was polished wood with paintwork picked out in gold leaf. To port there was a beautiful table that could seat six at dinner, set in gimbals and so nicely balanced that anything placed on it stayed in position even with *Westward* sailing on her ear when racing. The whole of the after part of the interior, cabins included, was fitted out to the very highest standards of comfort even down to carpets, yet this

ship was the same one that had been called 'that racing machine'.

Forward of the saloon there were storerooms, two more spare cabins, the steward's pantry, galley, sailing master's cabin, petty officers' mess, cook and stewards' cabin, first and second hands' cabin and the crew's forecastle; without using the saloon settees, *Westward* could sleep thirty-two crew at one time. Sails not stowed on deck ready for use were sent down via a large hatch forward of the mainmast into the hold; tanks, piping, spare gear and stores, and later the engine and shafting were also carried in the very considerable space below the sole. The accommodation area forward of the mainmast was accessible from the saloon, but the crew and officers used two steep companionways, one in the fo'castle which came out on deck just aft of the anchor windlass, the other in the common area between the officers' cabins.

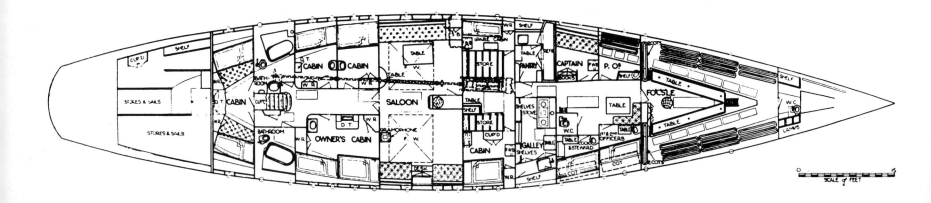

# Chapter 9

The work of preparing the schooner for racing was begun the day before the event. The two motorboats and their davits, gangplanks, etc were landed to save weight and to clear the decks of all obstructions. The outside of the hull was washed from stem to stern and all decking scrubbed, brightwork leathered and brass polished. On the day of the race she was a hive of activity. After an early breakfast the galley fires were drawn, which meant no more hot meals until after racing was ended for the day, and the crew mustered on deck at 0630. The rowing dinghy was lashed upside down on deck for emergency use, and all loose deck gear lashed down, or it would soon be lost over the side when the yacht started to heel. A start was then made on lubricating and cleaning all the brass blocks and fairleads, which had to be screwed back into their deck plates. In the forecastle all the pipe cots were lashed back against the ship's side and the two fore-and-aft tables pushed up to the deckhead and held there with splitpins; the centre floorboards were lifted ready for up-anchoring and the rest of the forecastle was used as a vast sail bin for the headsails. The next routine was to get all sails stopped with 'rotten cotton' prior to racing, so that they could be hoisted and broken out quickly as required. After checking all standing rigging and running gear the crew were stood down and given time for a rest before the really hard work of racing began.

As soon as the guests came aboard they were each given a job to do under the eye of various seamen. The only ones excused were the women, but as far as the men were concerned they worked their passage, and Davis would have no slackers. As a schooner is very hard to work, particularly when racing, T B used regularly to give young men in the Royal Navy an opportunity to see what racing was like in the big class yachts, and as far as I know he was the only owner who offered this experience.

Referring to the point about 'no slackers', I quote from a letter I received from a Commander, RN who had been one of the team.

*Hoisting sails – hands, steward, mates and owner (Alex Cochran)*
*tailing on the halyards.*

'I mainly recall the rather forceful language used by the owner. As boys, in our white duck suits, we were under the control of two lieutenants who were dressed in yachting rig. Soon after arrival on board off Cowes, preparations were being made to hoist sails, etc and the halyards were well and truly manned by the eager boys, when a roar was heard from aft: "Get off your bloody backsides—you're here to work, not for a bloody holiday." Looking round, we found it was directed to our two divisional officers, who happened to be sitting comfortably on the hatch coaming.

'The next cause of an outburst was when, as I remember it, foresails or foretopsails were hoisted with cotton stops as the sail was hauled out of the locker along the deck. These cotton stops, normally put in with a single turn, parted as the sheets were hauled in at the precise time of rounding a buoy. Unfortunately, I presume one of our party made a good job by doubling up on one of the stops, with the result that as the sail was ordered to be broken out, only half the stops parted; apart from the language which followed, we were very impressed to see a crewman go very quickly up the mast and down the luff of the sail with a knife.

'It may seem strange that after an interval of forty-five years I cannot remember very much about the races, only the language of the owner. Possibly it was because it would have been, at the age of sixteen, the first time I had been in the company of a millionaire.'

Racing *Westward*, particularly in heavy weather, was very hard work indeed and by the end of the day the whole crew was exhausted. As this was in the days before suitable winches the crew and all male guests under the age of forty-five manned the mainsheet together. To sweat this in after each reaching leg took approximately ten minutes. The ratio between the blocks on the mainsheet was twelve to one, so that each foot of sheet heaved in brought the main boom in one inch. One of the mates had the responsible duty of operating the stopper, which clamped the sheet each time it was pulled in, until the time came to make it fast at the bitts, and when this operation was completed the crew and guests were only too thankful to be allowed to lie on the weather deck and get their breaths back.

When sailing, one is used to hearing the order 'Ready about—lee-ho' as she is about to change tacks and as the helm is actually put over. In *Westward* the order was 'Women below, ready about, lee-ho.' This was a wise precaution as most of the female guests aboard had not a clue about sailing, and T B had enough on his hands without retrieving women from the lee scuppers: this chore was left to Miss Davis, who so I am told was a very efficient sheepdog and was always the last down

the companionway and the first up, after all gear was sheeted home and the schooner was on her new course.

Putting *Westward* about was a far more complex operation than on the big cutters: not only was there much more gear to handle, but the foretopsail (the upper sail set behind the foremast above the gaff foresail) needed constant attention when tacking, for it was of an unusual type beloved by T B. It was jib-headed and had to be changed on each tack; in fact two such sails were carried, one on each side of the foresail and its gaff tackles, and sliding up and down on jackstays. When one was hoisted its halyard was flaked down, and when she went about that topsail was let go and the other hoisted; these two sails set very well, as their shape was not interfered with by the gear for the gaff, but meant a lot of extra work. The headsail sheets were double-ended; the slack would be taken in on one leg and then a fourfold purchase hooked onto the other with eight hands or so on the tail. In a breeze this wasn't enough to get the sail hard in, so one of the mates would come up behind the last man and strop another fourfold purchase onto the sheet. With some more men on the new tail, the sail would be brought in further until the first gang could peel off and get on to the final purchase, working luff on luff.

Yachtsmen today have no conception of the noise created by tacking a schooner of the size of *Westward*: all orders had to be shouted, to be heard above the roar of a third of an acre of flogging canvas augmented by the rattling of blocks and sheets as the strain was taken off the running rigging. Once over on the new tack all would be peace again, except for the constant roar of the bow wave and water flowing along the lee scuppers.

*Sail changing during a race out past one of the Solent forts. The crew have just handed the jib topsail, and another is already stopped and being passed forward and hanked on. The photograph also shows the bowsprit rigging, its forged collar, a hawsepipe opening in the deck, and one of the two massive bolts taking the backwards thrust of the spar.*

*Breaking out a big jib topsail from its stops, as crew and guests haul in the sheet. The sail it replaces is being stowed on the bowsprit. (1931)*

To indicate more about how a big schooner was handled when racing, I quote from a letter sent to me by Frank S Beck, one of the permanent crew under Davis in *Westward*.

'Going about in *Westward* was very like any other yacht. The crew were not enough to tend everything, and the guests were told off by Mr Davis to help. There was a crewman on each sheet and the guests who were helping would be told by the crew which sheet to go to for going about, i.e. the sheet that wanted pulling in before turning up [into the wind]. The lee side sheet could be managed by the crewman.

'The bad one was the foretopsail, which had a separate sail for each tack. On "Lee-oh" the lee halyard was let go and the sail left to come down with a run. Should anyone be stupid enough to have a foot in a bight of halyard, he went up the mast till the sail hit the deck; when the weight was off he then dropped to the deck (this had happened the year before I joined). It was then a race against time to get the weather sail hoisted before she was on the next tack with everything drawing. Headsails sometimes had to be freed, and the bowspritendsman stood by for this.

'The hardest thing was coming on the wind at a mark after running. First there was the spinnaker and the spinnaker boom to take in, then nearly all hands were wanted to get the mainsheet in, because once the main was full you'd never get it hard in, and if you had to luff to complete this T B was not pleased and you would hear him all over the Solent! This left other sheets shorthanded and a real workup to harden in.

'The spinnaker boom was manhandled into position then lifted with the topping lift; the sail hoisted, then

*Setting the spinnaker. A man is standing on the foremast truss to clear the sail until it is set and filled.*

pulled by an outhaul to the end of the boom. Sometimes it had to be guided by a man in the fore-crosstrees, to avoid its fouling the topmast staysail or yankee jib topsail. Preventers were always used to stop any lift.'

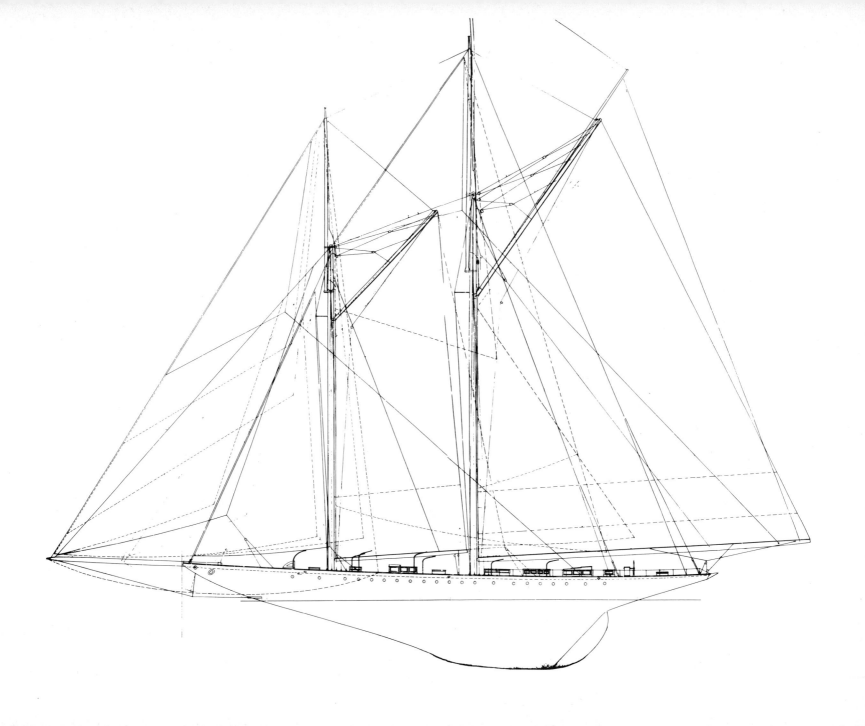

# Chapter 10

Sailmakers who fifty years ago catered for racing yachts were few and far between and consequently, and probably quite unintentionally, they were surrounded with a certain mystique. As T B Davis wanted to try out some new ideas with regard to sails on *Westward*, he decided to make them himself, which caused many raised eyebrows in the yachting world at the time. He acquired part of an old brewery in Jersey, which he converted into a sail loft and rigging shed. Not only did this find work for the crew during the winter months, but they soon became experts in the art of sailmaking. (One might say that T B showed the way that so many have followed, for sailmakers have sprung up like mushrooms all over the world, and as far as I know, none of them are starving.)

On a nice long run downwind, preferably in a Force 3 or 4, *Westward* could set ten sails, as photographs by Beken of Cowes prove. Talking of Frank Beken, who together with his son must surely be acknowledged as the greatest marine photographers of all time, he once said that 'to photograph *Westward* gives me the greatest pleasure, due to her matchless beauty'—praise indeed. He apparently knew T B well and sailed in the schooner on several occasions. Sailing off the wind with everything flying she was a very fine sight: forward of the foremast she set a forestaysail (on a stay from the stemhead to the top of the lower section of the foremast), outside that a jib, on a stay from the bowsprit end to the same point on the foremast, and then a jib topsail on the foretopmast stay which also ran down to the bowsprit end. A 'one-buttock' spinnaker was set out to the windward side of the outer headstay, rather than around everything in the modern fashion. Alternatively, a somewhat flatter masthead balloon jib that was nearly as large could be set to leeward and sheeted to the end of the foresail boom. On the after side of the foremast were the gaff foresail, fore topsail, small Queen staysail, and either a donkey sail (or mule) or a deeper and larger version known as a fisherman staysail. The head of this huge reaching and running

*Running under a balloon jib set from the masthead. Westward acquired an unusually high main topmast around 1928 which was kept until 1932. It required the additional spreaders and staying shown here, but allowed the main topsail to be set without a jackyard and its attendant weight and complication.*

sail was hoisted to the triatic stay between the tops of the two upper masts and its forward corner made fast to a downhaul on the foremast; and the free clew was sheeted well aft to the main boom. The gaff mainsail and main topsail set above it made up the ten sails. How often *Westward* was allowed to wear her full party dress I don't know, but she must have been a fantastic sight, and from contemporary accounts, she was recognizable from a long way off.

During the afternoon, and when the yacht was off the wind and therefore sailing upright, it was the custom for Miss Davis to arrive on deck with a cake stand loaded with small triangular cucumber sandwiches with the crusts cut off. These were handed round to the guests and young naval officers, who after all their exertions in the sea air were as hungry as hunters; this was a subtle form of torture, as they had to watch their ratings and the yacht's crew lacing into large doorsteps of bread, butter and jam. It must have made a profound impression on them, as several naval officers who sailed on *Westward* in the past have told me the story of the cucumber sandwiches.

Among those who often sailed with Mr Davis in *Westward* were Lord Jellicoe and his family. He was a very good yachtsman, and often took the schooner's wheel when racing. I remember that he made a great impression on me as a small boy, for I had been told that he was the only person in the world who could lose World War I in an afternoon (presumably because he had command of the Grand Fleet, and if he made a mistake in strategy and allowed the Kaiser's Imperial Fleet to beat us, we were finished).

Anyone who thinks that yachting is nothing more than an excuse for a lot of social junketing should

have gone out when it was really blowing. On such occasions the socialites and chattering women were left ashore, with the exception of Mrs Davis, who bravely came to sea and loathed every minute of it (the King on many occasions had rebuked T B for allowing this to happen). *Westward* would be stripped for action, carrying only foresail and main, forestaysail and jib, though the jib topsail and main topsail were usually set up tightly furled in stops in case the wind should slacken. Although it was possible to reef the gaff sails, this was seldom done, probably as it did not reduce their height or area very greatly; taking off the topsails was the first stage, and setting the smaller sized headsails. Rig of the day was oilskins with a towel inside the collar and a sou'wester; this attire worked well when you were perpendicular, but once you lay on the deck, which you did most of the time, you soon got drenched to the skin. Protective clothing has advanced a long way in fifty years, thanks to World War Two, the Submarine Service and ocean racing.

Attached to the port and starboard bulwarks was a safety line which the crew lying on the deck held on to, to save themselves from sliding across the canting surface into the water cascading along the lee scuppers,

White Heather II, Britannia *and* Westward *racing in 1926.* Britannia *had a new 40 ft hollow topmast socketed into a solid Oregon pine lower mast (the topsail jackyard was kept) and other alterations designed by William Fife. This rig was structurally a success, but twice took charge in strong winds, when she became unmanageable, and she was withdrawn from the latter part of the season. The yacht partly obscured by (7) is probably* Lulworth, *ex* Terpsichore. *These four, with* Shamrock IV, *made up the Big Class of that year.*

*Running. The foretopsail is being hoisted. Since it was set on a jackstay and sheeted to the end of the gaff, it was fairly easy to handle and could be re-set on the lee side of the gaff tackles. (T B had two topsails, set one on each side of the foremast, which could be switched when changing tacks.) The main topsail, when set with a jackyard and club as shown, or even when jib-headed on the extended topmast which* Westward *had for a short period, was more troublesome.*

and no one was allowed to move unless ordered to carry out some specific task. (Yacht hands were occasionally lost overboard, usually when racing, and their recovery was unlikely: few could swim, oilskins were stiff and heavy, and none wore lifejackets.) *Britannia* and *Westward* being excellent sea boats loved this kind of weather, but the wiser J Class yachts stayed at their moorings. Those that ventured out usually had a miserable time, for not only did their slim hulls slice through everything, turning the decks into a half-tide rock, but they never knew when their very expensive masts would collapse over the side, usually ruining the sails as well.

T B was never happier than when it was really blowing: he would stand at the wheel soaked through, with Alf Diaper beside him, ready should an extra hand be needed to hold it and looking anxiously at the straining canvas and bar-taut rigging, hoping to God that all would hold together, for her owner would never spare *Westward* but drive her harder than ever. Quite oblivious of everyone around, he would talk to her as if she were human—'Come on old girl, you can do better than this,' he would say, and in fact *Westward* was one of the few things he never swore at. It was never her fault, only himself and the crew.

As a change from heavy weather racing, in 1930 T B left the usual British coastal regattas after having only raced fourteen times (and gained five firsts, two seconds and three thirds), and pointed *Westward's* bows in the direction of the Mediterranean. As far as I can ascertain this was not a particularly happy venture as far as racing was concerned, though great fun socially. The passage to the Mediterranean had its moments, due to the fact that Alf Diaper, expert that he was around the racing buoys, found the Bay of Biscay a very large and lonely place. Not being able to converse with the Portuguese fishermen, it was left to the boatswain, an ex-RN chief yeoman of signals by the name of Smith, to contact each merchant vessel in turn to get accurate positions. As *Westward* encountered strong north-easterlies and had been rigged with a squaresail for the passage, she romped along, and made very fast time as far as Gibraltar. After stopping at Marseille for water and provisions, she arrived at Cannes to find the Davis family waiting for her.

The actual racing, such as it was, can best be described by a French correspondent who attended this regatta.

'The Riviera season has been notable for the reappearance in these waters for the first time for many years of a first class racer in the shape of Mr Davis's schooner *Westward*. Unfortunately she only had the ex-19 Metre yawl *Corona* and the large cruising schooner *Ailee* as competitors, but with this lead once given, others may accompany her next year, for *Britannia*, *Satanita* and *Ailsa* used to be regular visitors. A disagreeable feature of some of the racing was the number of fouls which occurred; added to this, certain Sailing Committees seem to have little idea of the elementary racing rules. Professional helmsmen have been blamed, but when "amateurs" demand payment before going afloat, and when an amateur helmsman shifts a mark before the race and keeps its new position strictly to himself, there can scarcely be said to be much between them.'

*Marjorie Davis (facing camera) and guests*

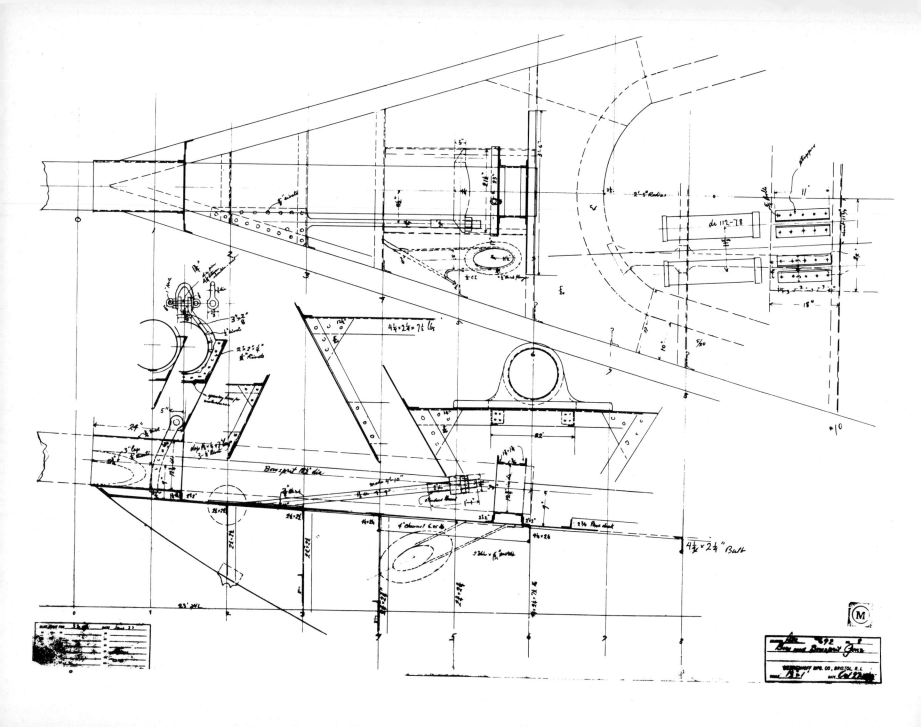

# Chapter 11

Yacht racing could be an exhausting occupation for the crews, not only because they were expected to give of their very best at all times when competing, but the ships had to be sailed, regardless of weather, round the coast from one regatta to the next. During the season between June 9 and September 1 the big yachts visited Harwich and Southend for the Down Swin races, Deal and Dover, the Solent, Hunters Quay, Gourock, Rothesay and Largs on the Clyde, Belfast Lough and Dublin Bay, Falmouth, Plymouth, Cowes, Ryde, Southsea, Bournemouth, Weymouth, and the West Country regattas at Brixham, Torquay and Dartmouth, and were always expected to arrive on time, making good the wear and tear of racing en route. This practice continued between the wars, but dated from the latter part of the century. The visiting big class made racing into something more spectacular and interesting for the general public, and capped the programme of events for local classes of smaller yachts; town regattas were a major event for both resorts and sailing centres.

Like any other boat, *Westward* had her anxious moments, and strange to relate the two incidents mentioned here were due to T B Davis's love of anchoring, and both took place in the Solent. The first occasion was when he went close inshore and dropped his hook in Totland Bay. During the night the gentle southerly wind swung round to the north-west and started to really blow. It was a very dark night with no moon, and T B finding himself on a lee shore with no engine and no room to claw off due to the rocks near by, did the only thing possible: he dropped his second anchor, let out a lot more chain, and prayed that the anchors would hold. Unfortunately, when *Westward* lay back on her cables in her new position closer to the shore, she found herself over a strand of firm sand and started to pound as low water approached. This went on for a long time, shaking her from keel to topmast, but the Herreshoff Manufacturing Co. had done their work well and she sustained no damage to her hull, though a lot of crockery and some glass on board was either shattered or cracked.

The second occasion was not so serious, just very annoying. When racing out of Cowes, T B had a favourite place where he always used to drop his anchor. It was well out in the Roads near the Squadron starting line, and he had anchored in this exact spot for years. When getting the anchor up prior to racing, it refused to come, with the chain straight up and down and bar-taut, and the language, so I am told, was as spectacular as the fireworks on the last Friday night of Cowes. The long-suffering harbour master rose to the occasion as usual and went across to the Guard Ship, who seeing *Westward* in trouble sent over their diving team. As time was ticking away and yachts were not allowed to race without an anchor and chain, everyone was on tenterhooks, particularly as the divers were having great trouble in getting down to the cause of the obstruction due to the turbulence of the tidal stream. At last the anchor was cleared and *Westward* got away before the ten minute gun was fired, thanks to the Navy or because, one might say, 'one good turn deserves another'.

After swinging on several tides, the schooner had wound her chain round the fluke of a huge anchor half buried on the seabed. During the winter this anchor was salvaged and found to weigh over four tons and have fifty fathoms of chain attached. Where it came from and who it belonged to is a mystery that has never been solved, but it had been down there for a very long time, and it was extraordinary that *Westward* had never fouled it before, having anchored there for so many years.

As part of Cowes Week the Naval Guard Ship besides providing divers in an emergency also held an annual dance on board. This had to be paid for by the officers themselves, on a sliding scale according to their rank: a lieutenant who received £24 per month was relieved of about £12 or two weeks' pay, and the Admiralty, though very keen on showing the flag, never paid a penny towards the expense. To make matters even more difficult, the many parties and the well known hospitality extended by the yacht clubs during the Week attracted those who were more interested in the social life than the sailing events. On one occasion the Guard Ship had eighty gatecrashers on board, all attacking the food and drink like hungry gannets. When the next vessel was detailed off for this duty at Cowes, the captain, who must have been a very brave man, wrote to the Admiralty and objected to the ever-increasing cost to officers, and was sent a grant of £75 to help defray expenses. This captain also sent out proper invitations, and stationed two lieutenants at the gangway to turn back the many gatecrashers without invitation cards; realizing that their bluff had been called, they soon passed the word round and caused no more trouble.

*Westward leading Britannia in a 1927 race. During the previous winter Britannia had been re-rigged with a one-piece Marconi mast, replacing the socketed topmast built in 1926. The jackyard was dispensed with, although the yard or club carrying the foot of the topsail above the gaff was kept; such topsails were known as 'yardless jackyarders'. The very wide low spreaders were later replaced by multiple spreaders of narrower span. These and other alterations were largely necessitated by changes in the measurement and rating rules. Westward adopted the 'yardless jackyarder' form of main topsail a year later, setting it on a taller but still separate topmast.*

The day before one dance several officers went aboard *Westward* and asked T B to attend: particularly as he was so good to the Navy they would like to have a chance to repay his hospitality. He turned the invitation down, saying 'I know you boys have to pay for that bloody dance out of your own pocket so I shall not come, but if you would like to ask my daughter and promise to look after her, I know she would be delighted to come', and this was agreed to.

The Naval dance had over the years developed into a set pattern. King George V, unlike his father, came to Cowes to sail and not for the social life, and as Queen Mary disliked boats it was the practice for the King to

send someone from the aristocracy to represent them. After being received by the senior officer present they would seat themselves at the end of the quarterdeck surrounded by potted plants and proceed to hold court with great efficiency, constantly surrounded with people wishing to pay their respects.

The two lieutenants receiving the guests and repelling gatecrashers were told to keep a good watch on *Westward*, and as soon as Miss Davis was seen approaching the word was passed round. Every officer who could detach himself without appearing rude mustered at the gangway, where every seaman who could use a bosun's pipe was also assembled. As soon as she came up the gangway the trilling of the many bosun's pipes even competed with the Marine band. Conversation stopped abruptly among the potted plants: had the Monarch after all decided to come on board? This query was soon answered, as Miss Davis, a slip of a girl, resplendent in her ball gown, stepped cheerfully onto the quarterdeck, and I am told that the expressions among the potted plants had to be seen to be believed.

After the party, the battleship received only four thank-you letters and one gentleman looking for his wife's missing glove. One of the notes was from T B, thanking the officers, on behalf of his daughter, for a splendid evening. For the benefit of many senior Naval officers who have asked 'What happened to that damn pretty Davis girl, I think her name was Marjorie?', she married a surgeon, Alexander Simpson-Smith, in 1939 in the quaint little Dartmouth church of St Petrox. During the war her husband became a lieutenant colonel in the RAMC and was taken prisoner at Tobruk in 1942, and was shot under tragic circumstances while trying to escape after seeing that all his casualties had

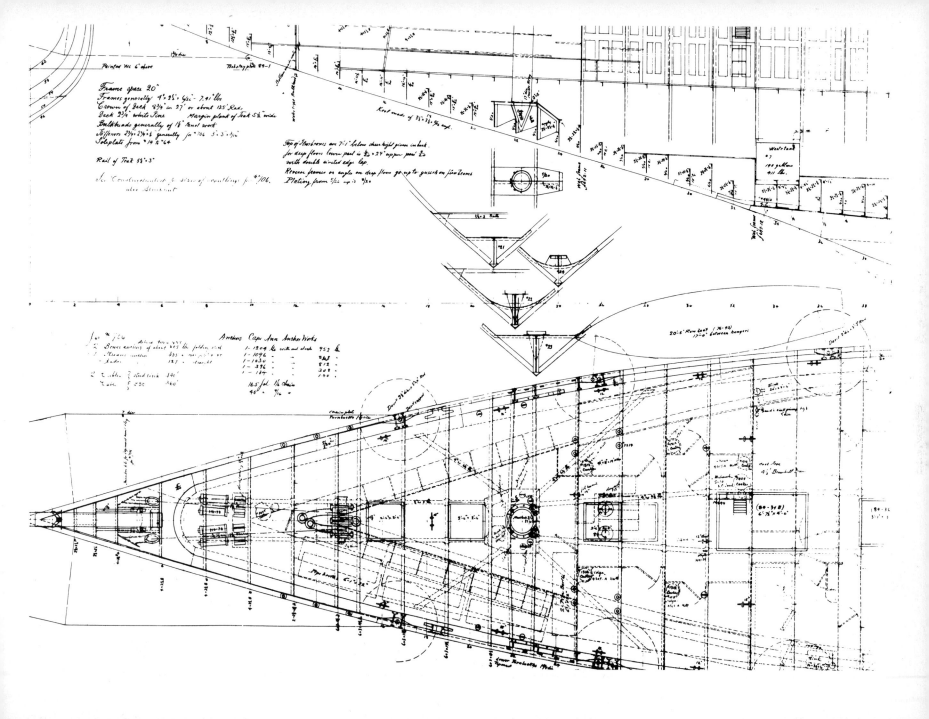

been taken care of. Mrs Simpson-Smith now lives with her sister in the Channel Isles. (There is no prize for guessing the name of their house.)

The King was genuinely fond of 'old Davis', as he called him, and on occasions would take him in for tea at the Squadron, much to the consternation of some of the older members, but as his host was Admiral of the club there was little that they could do about it. After one of these meetings T B was taken back to *Westward* in a steam pinnace. The young midshipman in charge made an error of judgement while coming alongside the schooner, due to the strong tidal eddies which every yachtsman out of Cowes knows about. After the second attempt T B said, 'Good god, boy, are you a Naval officer or a bloody farmer?' The midshipman reversed the pinnace clear of *Westward*, turned to T B and said, 'Mr Davis, Sir, you may be the captain when you are aboard *Westward*, but aboard this pinnace I am the captain—so shut up!' T B was so delighted that he told the King that there was nothing wrong with the Royal Navy so long as they went on producing young men of such spirit.

*Schooner weather for a reefed-down Big Class:* Westward *(5),* Candida *(K8),* White Heather II *(7),* Cambria *(K4),* Britannia *(1),* Lulworth *(6).* Westward *has furled all top-sails and is down to two headsails. Her extended main topmast compares with the mast height of the cutter* Candida. *This 1930 Solent race illustrates the practice of classing together yachts built in different years to different rules and subsequently modified:* Westward, *a 1910 Herreshoff schooner;* Britannia *(1893),* White Heather *(1907) and* Lulworth *(1920), gaff cutters;* Candida *and* Cambria, *launched 1928 and 1929 and Bermudian rigged.*

When cruising between regattas, one of Davis's favourite ports of call on the south coast was Fowey in Cornwall. Not only was Captain Collins, the harbour master, very attentive and always moored him fore and aft off Place Point, thus giving the local population a first class view of a splendid schooner, but T B found the depth of water at Fowey a refreshing change from St Helier, where *Westward* had to take the bottom on every tide.

On one occasion he and his wife went to tea with the Treffry family who lived in the district, and half way through tea Mr Davis remarked, 'Very poor quality milk you have, Mrs Treffry, can't be Channel Island milk'—the sort of remark that is difficult to follow. Some months later, when the tea party had long been forgotten, there was a phone call from the dock master at Southampton to say that there was an in-calf Jersey heifer, with a label round its neck which read 'To the Treffry family of Fowey with the compliments of T B Davis of Jersey', and would they please come and collect it as soon as convenient. It became the basis of the Place herd of Jersey cows, and from then on there were no more complaints about the milk.

Dartmouth was another favourite anchorage, and *Westward*'s frequent visits became longer as the years rolled by. T B finally rented a house just above the Kingswear ferry stage which had once belonged to the Captain of the *Cutty Sark*. The following yarns were told to me when I was researching *Westward*'s time on the Dart, by Captain Griffiths, the harbour master for many years. A professional seaman himself, he was inordinately proud of his river and liked everything to be done in a shipshape fashion; no doubt he was

86

subconsciously aware of the college flying the White Ensign on the hill overlooking the comings and goings about the river. Visitors were welcome, provided they did exactly as they were told.

Through the grapevine, Captain Griffiths had heard that Davis was about to bring *Westward* into Dartmouth and would no doubt anchor, and he was ready for her. In due course she arrived with her boat *Urda* under the long counter pushing her along. Davis was halfway down the companionway with just his hand sticking out, and the sailing master was in command. The crew were ready to let go the anchor, and as she came in near the correct position the harbour master ran along parallel with *Westward*, and shouted to the sailing master, 'When I tell you, let go your port anchor and I'll tell you when to let go your starboard one.' At this, Davis leapt up on deck and said 'Who the bloody hell are you to tell me what I'm going to do and what my ship is? What the bloody hell do you think you are?' Captain Griffiths shouted straight back at him, 'Either you bloody well anchor when I tell you, as I'm the harbour master, or you can bugger off out to sea. We don't want you and your bloody boat in here. Either you do as I tell you, or you can bugger off out of it.' This somewhat surprised old Davis, who said, 'Who the hell do you think you are? I'll look after my ship. I'm trained in deep sea, I've got an Extra Master's ticket, and I know what I'm doing. You're just the bloody harbour master on a little river like this.' From his launch Griffiths shouted back, 'And I've got an Extra Master's ticket like you have, you bugger, and also in sail. So either piss off or do as I tell you.' He then pushed the point home with, 'If you're a deep water man, you ought to bloody well know it's impossible to have two captains on a ship. Who's anchoring the bloody ship? You, or your sailing master?' When Davis said 'The sailing master is', Captain Griffiths shouted back at him, 'Right—well bugger off down below out of the way and let us get on with the job.' When anchoring was finished, Davis came up on deck and said, 'You're an awkward little bugger, aren't you? Come aboard,'— to be told, 'If you want me aboard, I'm an Extra Master—the same as you are. Extra Master in sail. And if you want me to come aboard, you'll treat me as an Extra Master and put the bloody boarding ladder down. So treat me proper.'

He then went aboard and they went down into the saloon for a drink, and so began a very fine friendship that went on for many years.

To my gentler readers I apologize for the language, but this clash of two strong personalities is interesting, for if one is a lion of a man, strong mentally and physically as well as being very rich, it is easy to become surrounded quite unintentionally with 'yes men'. Such stories are numerous in connection with Davis, who had fought his way up in a rough world and knew this only too well: he hated 'yes men' and admired people who would stand up to him, whether business rivals, midshipmen or harbour masters.

After *Westward* had been there for some weeks, Davis decided that he would like to go on a buoy. Though normally he never moored to buoys because he never trusted the links down by the sinker, he had already been told that all the Dartmouth moorings were looked after not just by the harbour master, but also lifted regularly by the Navy who had the necessary tackle, and that they were all in prime condition. As Davis couldn't bring himself to ask the harbour master direct,

he got in touch with a friend of his, a Mr Dennis of the Dartmouth Coaling Company, and asked if he could get the harbour master to let him have a mooring. When Mr Dennis asked the harbour master, the reply was, 'Davis gets the same treatment as everyone else. If he wants a mooring, he can come and ask for it himself.' This T B couldn't bring himself to do, and so *Westward* remained at anchor for another four or five weeks. When eventually he did go along, looking somewhat awkward and very cross, and asked 'What about a bloody mooring for *Westward*?' Captain Griffiths said to him, 'If you want a mooring, you can bloody well have one, man. There's four out there, which would you like?' 'Well, why the hell didn't you let me have one before?' 'Because you bloody well never asked, that's why.' After this little episode, all was peace again.

The next thing that I was told was a delightful story by Captain Griffiths about the King visiting Dartmouth on the royal yacht *Victoria and Albert*. He had apparently come in to see a ship which was being built further up the river, of interest because it was non-magnetic. As *Westward* was then lying at her buoy off the Philips & Sons yard and T B realized that the royal launch would have to pass him on the way up to see this ship, he went to the expense of completely re-rigging the whole of his crew in white ducks, and worked them and himself like a dog to get the ship so clean that anyone would be proud of it. The decks were as white as a hound's tooth, and when the harbour master went to visit he was made to take off his shoes before being allowed on deck. During the morning Davis had received a signal from the royal yacht asking him and his wife to attend that night for dinner, though he hadn't yet answered the signal. When the King came

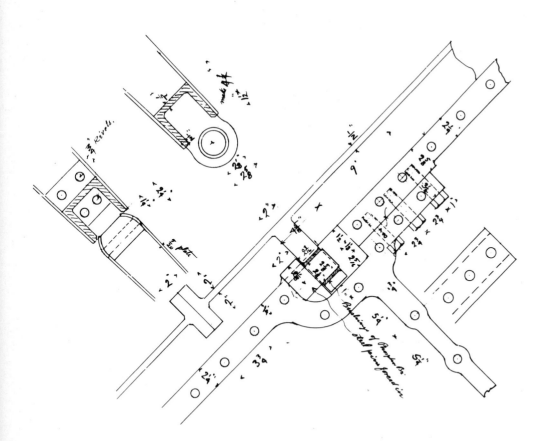

up in the royal barge everybody was lined up in an absolutely straight line just as if they were Naval personnel. Apparently old Davis hadn't much of a sense of humour on this occasion, but the King must have had, because as he approached *Westward* he turned his back on her and pretended to be studying Dartmouth Naval College on the other side of the river. He then passed on up-river to view the new ship, leaving T B deeply hurt and very angry. 'Stuck-up old devil' he was shouting around the deck. 'To think I've just made a bloody statue of him, and put it in my park in bloody Jersey. I'll uproot him. Yes I will, I'll uproot the old devil. Sod him. Sod everybody.'

Apparently he was eventually quietened down, and it was explained that this was really a practical joke, though the King thought his boat was absolutely beautiful. They quietened him down so much that he accepted for dinner that night, and as far as I know the statue of His Majesty is still in the Howard Davis Park in Jersey and in a perpendicular position.

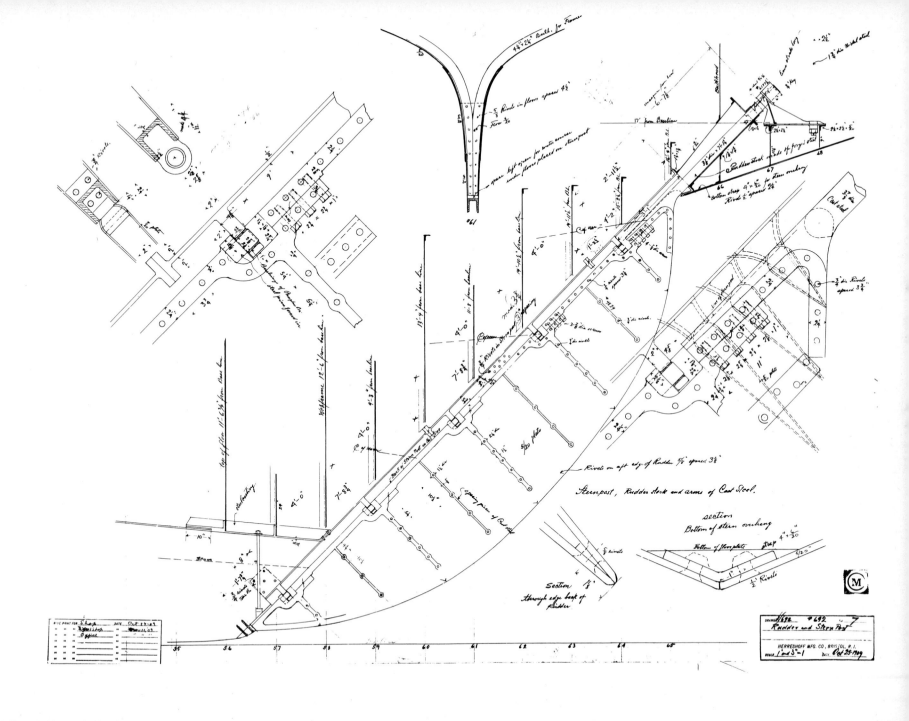

Sternpost, Rudder stock and arms of Cast Steel.

section
Bottom of Stern overhang

Section
Through edge back of Rudder

Rudder and Stern Post

HERRESHOFF MFG. CO., BRISTOL, R.I.
SCALE 1 and 3" = 1    DATE Oct 25-1909

# Chapter 12

We have talked at length about *Westward*, her crew and her owners, so I feel it is time that we discussed her ability to go out and win some races. To give a detailed account of each of her contests, rather like a golfer describing how he went round in two under his handicap, would soon become tedious, so I crave your indulgence if I only present some of the highlights, and wherever possible use quotations from experienced reporters of yacht racing.

During the 1920 to 1935 racing seasons *Westward* always had to race against the big cutters (except for the schooner *Susanne*, in the immediate post-war season, but instead of being odd man out she became accepted over the years. John Nicholson, in his book *Great Years of Yachting*, wrote:

'When my father visited the palace, he was most impressed by His Majesty's great knowledge of the details of the Big Class and amused at the King's remark that "Whatever we do to improve *Britannia*,

we must beat that damned schooner"—referring of course to *Westward*.' He continues: 'Many felt that the inclusion of that fine schooner in the cutter class was a pity, but there was no animosity among the owners. Her chances of winning under average conditions were remote, but in fine breezes with plenty of reaching she was a redoubtable competitor. She also inevitably raced on all days, many of which were more suited to the cutters, so she was accepted as a very sporting competitor.'

Major B Heckstall-Smith, reporting a race at Ryde, IOW on August 14, 1937 in which *Westward* beat *Shamrock V* by ten seconds, concurred.

'The King's yacht *Britannia* and *Westward* today sailed in their last race of the season. They competed with the rest of the Big Class in the Royal Victoria Yacht Club Regatta, *Westward* gaining a narrow victory by ten seconds from *Shamrock V*; *Velsheda* was third and *Britannia* fourth.

*Alf Diaper at the helm, T B Davis looking aloft.*

'*Westward* and *Shamrock V* had a keen race and the result hung in the balance for many miles. Although the wind was light throughout the day and the race began with a five mile turn to windward over a foul tide, the schooner kept her place among the cutters during the tacking and afterwards led the single-masted craft all round the course. Her speed in the gentle breeze was extraordinary.

'*Westward* is in many respects a remarkable vessel. She is the only remaining racing schooner in English waters, and she is the sole representative of the old gaff mainsail and jackyard topsail rig in notable racing classes—all the rest are rigged with the triangular Bermudian mainsail.'

This account is of interest in showing that even in light airs and closehauled *Westward* could hang onto, and beat, a really modern single-sticker like *Shamrock V*, twenty years her junior, thus disproving the statements that she was only good when reaching in a strong breeze.

Pride of place among her trophies, as far as T B Davis was concerned, was the Lymington Cup won in 1933. Not for anything spectacular about the race, but for the intrinsic beauty and gilding of the cup itself, which dates from 1864 at least, when it was won by the schooner *Aline*. (The cup and other trophies are on display in Jersey, and I was able to see it when over there researching this book.) For those interested in racing rather than cups, the corrected times were:

| | | | |
|---|---|---|---|
| *Westward* | 2.12.2 | *Candida* | 2.20.45 |
| *Britannia* | 2.15.24 | *White Heather* | 2.24.5 |
| *Astra* | 2.19.24 | *Shamrock V* | 2.25.40 |

In 1934, a different sort of event was seen in the Solent.

'Light winds marred the Royal Thames Y C endeavour to revive schooner racing with the race round the Isle of Wight last Friday, *Westward* proving an easy winner although the scratch boat.

'The starters were the 323 ton schooner *Westward*, the Canadian fishing schooner *Bluenose* of about 400 tons, Mr Walter Runciman's 161 ton *Altair*, Lord Stalbridge's 295 ton *Cetonia*, and Commander I B Kitson's 144 ton *Golden Hind*. The event for schooners

of 100 tons and upwards was arranged to mark His Majesty's Silver Jubilee year, which by the way is also the 160th anniversary of the foundation of the Royal Thames Yacht Club. The first prize was a cup to the value of £100 presented by Mr Allen C Messer, the second boat taking a prize of £50 and the third £25. The race was sailed on handicap; *Westward* was on scratch having to allow *Bluenose* 54 minutes, *Altair* 1 hour, 7 minutes, 24 seconds, *Golden Hind* 1 hour, 46 minutes, 12 seconds, and *Cetonia* 1 hour, 48 minutes, 54 seconds over a distance of about 54 sea miles.

'In 1921, '22, '23 and 1931 *Bluenose* won the International Fishermen's Trophy races between Halifax, NS and Gloucester, Mass., beating *Elsie, Henry Ford, Columbia* and *Gertrude L Thebaud*, so that with vessels of her own class she had a great reputation for speed. But fishing craft have never attained the speed of yachts, and when Major B Heckstall-Smith, Secretary to the YRA, was asked to handicap the *Westward* he decided that the racing yacht should give the fishing boat one minute per mile. After the start at eleven o'clock *Cetonia* was first over the line, followed by *Westward. Bluenose*, the Canadian schooner, with

*Britannia (K1),* Shamrock V *and* Westward *in 1932. Spinnaker poles have been set up, and a man sent aloft onto* Westward'*s mast truss ready to clear the sail as it goes up. Its head is visible just forward of the mast. Behind the schooner is* White Heather II, *re-rigged as a Bermudian cutter. At the close of the season her owner commissioned C E Nicholson to design and build* Velsheda, *to J class rules, using the old boat's keel lead.* Shamrock V *had been built as a J in 1930, also by Nicholson, as an America's Cup challenger for Sir Thomas Lipton.*

twenty-five members of the Island Sailing Club as additional crew, crossed the line over a minute late, closely followed by *Altair. Golden Hind* was last, *Oceana* did not start.

'In the beat to the eastward the schooners looked really lovely, a taste of what schooner racing might be. *Westward* went out ahead, while *Bluenose*, definitely not in her weather, managed to gain second place from *Altair*. The fleet had a foul tide through Sandown Bay until off Dunrose where the ebb set in, passing Ventnor Pier at the following times: *Westward* 1 hour, 25 minutes; *Altair* 2 hours, 15 minutes; *Bluenose* 2 hours, 17 minutes; *Golden Hind* 2 hours, 55 minutes; *Cetonia* 3 hours, 38 minutes.

'The wind going round to the southwest gave them a reach from St Catherine's Point to the Needles. Off St Catherine's *Cetonia* had overtaken *Golden Hind* before 6 p.m. Up the Solent a veering, lightening wind gave them a long, tedious run against the last of the ebb.

'*Bluenose*, not at her best in the light winds, had everything set of her own plus a borrowed spinnaker. This enabled her to hold *Altair*, but *Westward* still slipped ahead of them all and before 6 o'clock had been sighted from the Royal Guard Ship. The breeze fell to almost a calm as the sun went down, *Cetonia* and *Golden Hind* not yet having cleared the Needles. *Bluenose* could not quite catch *Altair* and finished third. Times were as follows:

|  | finish | corrected |
|---|---|---|
| *Westward* | 6.51.14 | 6.51.14 |
| *Altair* | 8.14.43 | 7.6.19 |
| *Bluenose* | 8.20.38 | 7.26.38 |

This endeavour to revive schooner racing failed, and no further attempt was ever made in this country.

One of the races that pleased T B Davis was when he won the King's Cup at Cowes on August 8, 1934, and this extract is taken from Major B Heckstall-Smith's report to *The Telegraph* of that date.

*King George V's yacht underwent substantial modifications in the course of her long career, of interest because they show the effects of successive rating rules and development in design. Westward, however, while skilfully and lovingly maintained, stood aside from this aspect of racing, competing on handicap and sailing hard against more modern yachts. In 1931 Britannia appeared with a new Bermudian rig designed by Charles E Nicholson, and other Big Class yachts made similarly drastic and costly alterations. She was given a new and shorter bowsprit, steepening the headsail luffs, and a new hollow one-piece mast. The boom was shortened, ending forward of the stern, and boom struts were added to counteract sagging. Removing 3 tons of gaff and gear from aloft allowed the compensating removal of 15 tons of ballast, lifting her in the water and increasing the freeboard. Inside ballast was then moved to the keel to achieve the required 15 ft draft, and the keel profile altered. The mainsail now measured 5400 sq ft out of a total sail area of 8700 sq ft; the sailplan height was 165 ft above deck and 124 ft from bowsprit end to mainsail clew. In 1932 the hull was re-coppered and the sail area cut to 8100 sq ft; Astria and Cambria had already established the value of reducing sail area to obtain a more beneficial rating without sacrificing speed. In 1933 the mast was stepped slightly further aft, but despite these measures, her performance during the season indicated that she was falling behind her rivals. (1933)*

'T B Davis won the King's Cup today with his splendid schooner *Westward*, defeating the whole class of cutters. Many onlookers declared that there were moments when she was doing fourteen knots. I believe this estimate to be justified. Mr Davis, with two sailmakers, made the whole of *Westward*'s suit of sails in his native island of Jersey, and the set and general contour of the schooner's canvas was not surpassed by any racing yacht at Cowes.

'So beautifully is this remarkable vessel balanced and trimmed that today, when reaching towards the finishing line at Cowes, a slim young girl, Miss Marjorie Davis, the owner's daughter, was steering her quite easily for the last few hundred yards of the race. This was for a brief period when the yacht was thundering along with her decks foaming in green water and spindrift flying from her lee rigging screws like smoke.

'The spectacle of the immensely powerful schooner when she crossed the line, received her gun, and won The King's Cup, travelling at thirteen knots with only the light hand of a girl upon the wheel, was most inspiring.'

|  | finishing | corrected |
|---|---|---|
| *Westward* (T B Davis) | 2.30.49 | 2.30.48 |
| *Velsheda* (W L Stephenson) | 2.34.24 | 2.33.52 |
| *Candida* (H A Andrewe) | 2.43.38 | 2.34.54 |
| *Astra* (H F Paul) | 2.45.21 | 2.38.37 |
| *Shamrock V* (C P Fairey) | 2.46.28 | 2.42.56 |
| *Britannia* (H M the King) | 2.49.30 | 2.43.58 |

In 1935 Britannia *came out with further modifications: forestaysail and quadrilateral jib instead of three headsails, still steeper stays, and a flat-topped 'Park Avenue' boom designed to stop the flow of air down off the mainsail and to allow it to assume its ideal aerodynamic curvature (it also tended to give the sail a too-tight leech). The emphasis was on improving light wind performance, but though she placed relatively well in fresh conditions, she was markedly slower in light airs and clearly being outclassed. In her last race, in Cowes Week, she and* Shamrock *were far behind in a brisk breeze. The royal yacht was withdrawn from the rest of the season's events and did not race again.*

This win by the twenty-four year old *Westward* so pleased her designer that he wrote a letter in his own hand to T B which I think may be of interest.

N G Herreshoff
Bristol, R I

August 17, 1934
Thomas B F Davis, Esq.
Care of National
Banks S.A. Ltd
London Wall

Dear Mr Davis,

A friend has sent me a cutting from the London *Telegraph* of August 8th, by B Heckstall-Smith, of *Westward*'s triumph in the race for the King's Cup and I want to send you my congratulations and say how pleased I am at the result.

It was *Westward*'s day and she proved her ability and the fine handling she is getting. The scene at the finish of the race when your daughter was steering must have been wonderful indeed and I wish I could have been there to see it.

Nicholson has turned out a beautiful vessel in *Endeavour*, and it looks like a real job to retain the America Cup this time. Mrs Herreshoff joins me in kindest regards to Mrs Davis and yourself, and I want to express my admiration at the skill you have displayed in the upkeep and fitting out of *Westward* with your crewmen.

Sincerely yours,
Nathanael Greene Herreshoff

Mrs and Mrs Davis had been over to meet Nat Herreshoff in America, and Nat paid T B the great compliment of taking him up to his 'holy of holies' where all the half-models of his famous designs were kept: he told him that the half-model of *Westward* was among this large collection, and that he could have it if he could recognize it. T B walked straight to it, and it is now a treasured possession of his descendants.

# Chapter 13

The 1935 season was sad in many ways for *Britannia* and *Westward*: the J Class boats were becoming much more efficient, and as light winds had characterized the whole season the latest Js performed as real flyers, with the result that the figures below make sorry reading.

| | starts | prizes | | | points |
|---|---|---|---|---|---|
| | | 1 | 2 | 3 | |
| *Endeavour* (T Sopwith) | 35 | 12 | 10 | 6 | 74 |
| *Astra* (H Paul) | 35 | 8 | 7 | 3 | 49 |
| *Velsheda* (W Stephenson) | 36 | 5 | 8 | 11 | 47 |
| *Yankee* (G Lambert) | 32 | 8 | 4 | 2 | 42 |
| *Candida* (H Andrae) | 28 | 2 | 4 | 3 | 19 |
| *Shamrock V* (C Fairey) | 34 | 0 | 2 | 7 | 11 |
| *Westward* (T B Davis) | 11 | 2 | 0 | 0 | 8 |
| *Britannia* (HM the King) | 20 | 0 | 0 | 0 | 0 |

Much as one hates to admit it, the time had come for the twenty-five year old schooner and the forty-two year old cutter to be put out to grass, like two faithful old hunters. *Britannia* went back to the loving care of Marvin's yard at Cowes and *Westward* sailed back to St Helier in Jersey, and the old boats never met again.

On the night of January 20, 1936 King George V died, quite suddenly, and the fate of *Britannia* was sealed, for the new King was more interested in golf than sailing. On July 10 she was scuttled, out in the Channel, halfway between St Catherine's Point and the Hurd Deep.

The death of King George V caused great distress to T B Davis; not only did he admire him tremendously but he had a genuine affection for him, and had already stated that the day *Britannia* finally hauled down her racing flag *Westward* would do the same. But he still had plans for his old schooner, and she was to be seen around the coasts of Europe for another twelve years.

St Helier Harbour seen at low water springs, with a maximum tide range of about 39 feet, is hardly the place to keep a 323 ton racing schooner with a very pronounced cut away forefoot and a draft of 16 feet 9 inches, but due to her excellent construction and the

*'Rat Corner' in St Helier, Jersey, where* Westward *took the bottom at low water. The wooden cradle under the forefoot kept her level.*

*Weighing anchor on the line (1935). From left:* Astra, 23 *Metre, designed by C E Nicholson in 1928 for Mr Hugh Paul;* Endeavour I, *J Class America's Cup challenger in 1934, designed by Nicholson for Mr T Sopwith;* Westward; Candida, 23 *Metre built in 1927 for Mr H Andrae;* Velsheda, *built by Nicholson for Mr W L Stephenson in 1933 and the only British J boat not intended as a Cup challenger. The two Js have set genoa jibs, one of the features that made them efficient in conditions such as this.*

care of her crew she came to no harm. A special cradle was fabricated to support her overhanging bow when she took the bottom. The part of the harbour wall that she had made her own rejoiced in the name of 'Rat Corner' and was adjacent to the St Helier Yacht Club. On this quay T B made the new spars for *Westward*, having already gone over to America to select the two trees that the masts were to be fashioned from, after receiving exorbitant quotations from yacht yards in England for the job. This was a mammoth undertaking for himself and his crew, but quite undaunted they set to work. T B had built a large business empire, so why should he not build his own large masts? The finished spars were a first class piece of workmanship that he was inordinately proud of. With the topmast I believe the total height of the mainmast was 143 feet. The two old topmasts were not thrown away: one became the flagstaff for the St Helier Yacht Club; the other ended up in the seven ton auxiliary gaff cutter *Onyx* that still dries out on every tide in St Aubin's harbour.

Once *Westward's* racing days were over, her owner turned his attention towards using the yacht for cruising, and with this in mind decided that she must be fitted with auxiliary power. As usual, the work was to be carried out by himself and the crew under the supervision of an expert from Ailsa Craig Ltd. The engine to be installed was a six-cylinder Ailsa Craig DDR6 diesel $4\frac{1}{8} \times 5\frac{1}{2}$ inch rated at 48 h.p. (maximum 72 h.p.) with a three-bladed 28 inch diameter and 21 inch pitch propeller turning at half engine speed. Davis stipulated that all external gear should be removable leaving the hull completely flush, so that his children could race her again if they should so wish. Furthermore, the machinery was to be entirely installed under the

*T B Davis and his crew shaping new spars*

accommodation floor; two five ton water tanks built in abaft the mainmast could not be removed; the sail stowage in the hold forward of the mainmast could not be interfered with; and not more than one steel hull frame was to be cut and it would have to be made good by bridging.

These requirements demanded considerable ingenuity from Ailsa Craig. A special stern gland with a flush outer surface was designed and the A-bracket supporting the shaft was made to bolt to stiffening plates riveted inside the hull. The shaft coupling was in halves to be easily removable with the shaft and propeller so that the hole could be plugged for racing. The engine was placed forward of the main saloon in the crew area and near the centreline, with the shaft angled inwards from the quarter in order to obtain a satisfactory position for the propeller under the long fine run of the stern. The shafting had to be run through the port water tank in a tunnel, avoiding the internal baffle plates. Three triangular plates bolted to the frames carried the engine beds, forming a sort of shelf built out from the side of the hull with the starter battery underneath and 200 gallons of fuel in three triangular tanks alongside. The exhaust provided yet more problems, as under severe sailing conditions hardly any part of the hull was not at some time under water. In 1937, as the speed estimated by the makers proved optimistic, another engine of the same type and power was installed on the starboard side.

In 1936 *Westward* went on a four months' cruise to Norway and Sweden. Captain Paul was put in command; he was a professional seaman, rather than a sailing master, and I think I am right in saying that he had commanded one of the *Endeavours* when she crossed the Atlantic to America for the Cup races. When cruising, *Westward* worked under reduced rig, and a very reduced crew of only four ABs, two to each watch. The alteration in her sail plan made her difficult to handle, and in strong winds required two men to steer; she also became difficult to heave-to. With her cut away forefoot, her underwater profile only really started to develop draft aft of the foremast, so with nothing much under the water from there forward, the hull acted like a sail and she would pay off, given the slightest opportunity.

For some reason T B did not take passage in her. Perhaps he thought that two masters in one ship was not a good idea, so he followed by land in his Rolls, but used the schooner instead of hotels at all her stopping points, such as Gothenburg and Oslo.

During this cruise the wind blew hard from the southwest, and despite her reduced rig *Westward* flew along with the seas on her starboard quarter. The crew could not resist passing close to tramp steamers going in the same direction, with the yacht reeling off the miles at a steady ten or eleven knots. On the way back, as the wind had veered to the northeast they sailed through most of the Kiel Canal—the scene of her early incarceration—then returned to St Helier via Dover and St Peter Port, Guernsey.

Over the years *Westward* continued to go on short cruises. Her life had become far less strenuous, but this does not mean that she was being in any way neglected, for she was still maintained as carefully as ever. But her age was respected, and she was never driven as she had been when racing.

When World War Two was declared *Westward* found herself in Dartmouth and remained there for the period of hostilities, moored off the Philips & Son Ltd boatyard, and under the supervision of a Mr Dennis, managing director of the Dartmouth Coaling Co. and a friend of T B's. Davis did not sleep aboard *Westward* again. Most of his time was spent in South Africa, where he died in 1942 aged 75.

In his will the schooner was bequeathed to his family, but as there was no prospect of her ever being raced again, or cruised for that matter, the family offered her to three separate training establishments on condition that she was to be properly maintained, and not allowed to fall into decay and left to rot forgotten and unloved up some muddy creek, as has so often been the fate of many a lovely old boat. In postwar Britain, with shortages of facilities, materials and cash, no one was interested, and the final clause in T B Davis's will came into force: the destruction of this splendid old schooner.

The ship's launch *Urda* was given as a present to his friend Mr Dennis, and Mr Alec Philips at the yard was instructed to prepare *Westward* for scuttling in

*Lady Trent, a guest on board during the Norwegian Yacht Racing Centenary celebrations, with T B.*

Hurd Deep. The beautiful masts, T B's pride and joy, were cut off two feet above deck level, and she was stripped of everything except the fine wood panelling in the saloon and the keel lead. Three separate charges were placed in her bilges near the keel. The explosive to be used was of a new type, obtained from a nearby stone quarry and reported to be much more powerful than that normally used; attached to these charges were slow burning fuses which ran across the deck to protrude through the port scuppers.

When all was ready, this sad little procession sailed in command of Captain R Griffith, then the Dartmouth harbour master and an old friend of *Westward*'s late owner. The schooner was taken in tow by the tug *Portway* and headed out to sea for the last time. Captain Griffith told me the final story when we sat together in his garden shed at Stoke Fleming; as he was in charge of the navigation he had estimated that *Portway* would

tow *Westward* at about five knots and had worked out his ETA on that assumption; on clearing the coast the fog rolled in 'as thick as a bloody hedge' and they could not even see *Westward* astern. To make matters worse, the old tug *Portway* was having one of her off days, and Captain Griffith found that he could throw an empty cigarette packet over the side, walk smartly down the deck to the stern and still arrive before it did. By this trading schooner reckoning, he found that the funeral procession was travelling at about two and a half to three knots. All he had as a position check was the sound of the Weymouth mail steamer thrashing through the fog in the direction of the Little Russel Channel, bound for St Peter Port in Guernsey, away to starboard.

After a while Captain Griffith stopped the tug's engine to listen and *Westward* ranged up alongside through the mist, to see what was happening; at last

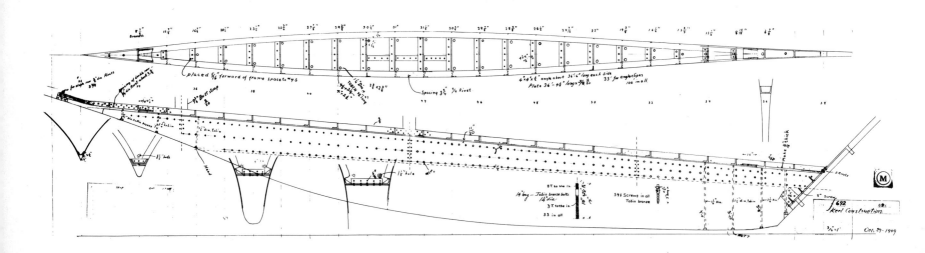

they heard the Casquets blowing, two blasts every sixty seconds, and before long visibility improved and he was able to get the bearing that he wanted so badly. In a position 5½ miles off and bearing 10° true from the Casquets light, in 94 fathoms of water, *Westward* was cast adrift. The tug came alongside, the explosives expert from the stone quarry lit two of the fuses and the harbour master the third, and *Portway* lumbered off at her best speed. The explosion was such that it was heard by a fishing boat working off the Skerries Rocks, for it rattled his wheelhouse windows. At 12.45 p.m. on July 15, 1947 *Westward* died.

The final indignity to be bestowed upon her was a tirade from the popular press, under the heading 'Famous Racing Yacht to be Destroyed, to Please a Dead Man's Whim'—totally disregarding all the efforts of the Davis family to find *Westward* a suitable home where she would have been appreciated and cared for.

To the watermen in Dartmouth she will long be remembered, for her vast spars have been cut down to make new masts and part of a derrick; her specially strong wire rigging, the blocks and best quality Italian hemp running gear were soon put to good use, and no doubt the anchor chains, sunk deep in the riverbed, have held many a moored yacht steady in a blow. But if you mention *Westward* to the older generation of seamen, they all say the same thing: 'Fine ship the *Westward*, but they should never have sunk her—for she had seventy-five tons of lead on her bottom and her keel bolts were made of solid bronze and they were as thick as your arm—God knows what that lot was worth!' As I walked away, I had the feeling that the ghosts of their ancestors, the famous ship wreckers of generations ago, were still not very far away.

So this is the end of the story of a beautiful schooner. She lies at peace, protected by the depth of water and the sluicing tides. For thirty-seven years she had graced the yachting scene and represented all that was best in design and workmanship, and she typified an era which will never be repeated.

*T B Davis racing* Westward

Appendix I

## *Westward* and *Britannia*

Those interested in the long rivalry between these two yachts might like to observe the following figures.

|  |  | starts | prizes | | | points | performance |
|---|---|---|---|---|---|---|---|
|  |  |  | 1 | 2 | 3 |  | figure |
| 1925 | Britannia | 36 | 6 | 0 | 6 | 30 | 0·83 |
|  | Westward | 29 | 8 | 2 | 4 | 40 | 1·39 |

In 1926 *Britannia* was withdrawn near the end of the season; during the winter of 1925, she had been drastically altered to get more speed in light airs, and this rig proved dangerous in strong gusty weather.

| 1927 | Britannia | 24 | 8 | 6 | 2 | 46 | 1·92 |
|---|---|---|---|---|---|---|---|
|  | Westward | 24 | 7 | 3 | 3 | 37 | 1·54 |
| 1928 | Britannia | 34 | 9 | 5 | 5 | 51 | 1·50 |
|  | Westward | 22 | 3 | 4 | 1 | 21 | 0·97 |

In 1929 *Britannia* was again a non-starter, due to the serious illness of King George V.

| 1930 | Britannia | 26 | 5 | 4 | 1 | 29 | 1·12 |
|---|---|---|---|---|---|---|---|
|  | Westward | 14 | 5 | 2 | 3 | 27 | 1·93 |
| 1931 | Britannia | 20 | 6 | 4 | 3 | 35 | 1·75 |
|  | Westward | 11 | 0 | 1 | 2 | 4 | 0·36 |
| 1932 | Britannia | 32 | 9 | 11 | 3 | 61 | 1·91 |
|  | Westward | 18 | 4 | 0 | 1 | 17 | 0·95 |
| 1933 | Britannia | 39 | 12 | 9 | 3 | 69 | 1·77 |
|  | Westward | 12 | 1 | 0 | 0 | 4 | 0·33 |
| 1934 | Britannia | 27 | 3 | 3 | 4 | 22 | 0·81 |
|  | Westward | 10 | 2 | 1 | 1 | 11 | 1·10 |
| 1935 | Britannia | 20 | 0 | 0 | 0 | 0 | 0·00 |
|  | Westward | 11 | 2 | 0 | 0 | 8 | 0·73 |

Appendix II

# The Benefactions of T B Davis

Davis's eldest son, Howard Leopold, was killed in World War One, and many of the public benefactions were given in his memory; the following is a list of some of Davis's gifts to Jersey and South Africa.

States Experimental Farm, a forty vergée farm presented to the States in 1928 for research and development of Jersey agriculture.

Howard Leopold Davis Scholarship Trust, instituted in 1933 to help promising Jersey boys to enter some form of Imperial Service.

Howard Davis Hall, Victoria College, opened in 1935 by the Prince of Wales. It contained a fine full-length portrait by J H Lander of King George V and a working replica of the famous Greenwich clock.

£50,000 donated to the Widows and Orphans Fund of the Company of Master Mariners.

*Howard Davis* Lifeboat   This was a powered boat, and at the time (1937) an innovation in lifeboat construction; it is not now stationed on the Island.

The Howard Davis Park   T B Davis purchased 'Plaisance', the former residence of the Falle family, and employed J H Colledge, the famous landscaper of gardens, to lay out the grounds as a public park. It contains a statue of King George V and a Hall of Remembrance.

St Luke's Church Hall commemorating his boyhood associations with this church, where he was a permanent member of the choir.

Glenham Hall Scouts Island HQ   The hall, named after his elder son, was built in New St James Place on a site given by the Trent family.

£25,000 donation for the assistance of the families of serving men during the Second World War.

Contributions to the Channel Islands Refugees Fund in the United Kingdom.

Howard College, Durban   A college of engineering built in 1931 for the University of Natal on a fifty acre site given to the Corporation.

*General Botha* Training Ship, presented to the Union of South Africa shortly after World War One. The ship was equipped to train one hundred British and one hundred Dutch cadets, and is now a shore-based institution.

Howard Davis War Fund, established at the outset of World War Two. The purpose of this £100,000 fund was to promote recruiting of British and Dutch soldiers in South Africa by ensuring that their dependants were provided for.

This list is incomplete, for T B Davis made countless other benefactions, large and small, most of which were never publicized.

# Drawings

*Westward* was hull no. 692, built 1909–10 by the Herreshoff Manufacturing Co. On some of the drawings there are references to hull no. 706 *Elena*, built largely from the same plans, though with slight alterations.